FENG SHUI TAROT

GUIDE BOOK TO THE FENG SHUI TAROT DECK

BY EILEEN CONNOLLY
AND PETER PAUL CONNOLLY

U.S. GAMES
SYSTEMS, INC

U.S. GAMES SYSTEMS, INC.
Stamford, CT 06902 USA

First Edition

CIP data is available

ISBN 1-57281-491-8

10 9 8 7 6 5 4 3 2 1

Printed in Canada

U.S. GAMES SYSTEMS, INC.
179 Ludlow Street
Stamford, CT 06902 USA
www.usgamesinc.com

For Lindy

TABLE OF CONTENTS

PREFACE

*F*eng Shui Tarot and the Feng Shui Tarot Deck are both collabo-
rative efforts from Eileen and Peter Paul Connolly. In this unique
presentation you will see how this best-selling Tarot deck translates
the Feng Shui imagery into the ancient language of Tarot. The deck
represents the first time these two schools have come together, thus
creating a new and exciting tool for the students of both Tarot and
Feng Shui.

The melding of Tarot and Feng Shui will hopefully open a wide
door of opportunity to the practitioners of both esoteric sciences.
Each of the respected theories can be comprehended by the individual practitioner of Tarot or Feng Shui without having to delve into or
infringe upon the other.

The reader of this deck has the choice to follow the rudiments
of either theory or both. The reader can elect to read and delineate
the spread with the focus entirely on the Tarot. The alternative
would be to use your knowledge and expertise using the Basic Form
School of Feng Shui to appreciate the depths that the Tarot can offer.

In my previous books I have personally chosen to use Christian
symbology, but I have decided not to reference Christianity in the
Feng Shui Tarot Deck in order to allow the reader to contemplate
their own symbology or spirituality.

Peter Paul and I have worked fastidiously to create the Tarot
deck and this guide book. The first task was to research the two
seemingly unrelated philosophies. Our goal was to identify the elements that would be compatible with each other, and that also
would provide the reader with a basic understanding of each of
these theories. From that point it was important to find the "key"
that would lock the Tarot and Feng Shui together to create the valid-

ity of the Feng Shui Tarot Deck. Once the structure became feasible, we then had to begin making solid plans to go ahead and realize our goal. My son now refers to me as the Tarot expert and I now refer to him as the Feng Shui authority on our project. Peter Paul had an enormous undertaking, that of creating a disciplined methodology into the beautiful artwork that you see in the Feng Shui Tarot Deck.

The reader will enjoy the sections written by Peter Paul. He takes you on a tour of understanding by explaining, in detail, how the basic relationship of these two skills makes a perfect marriage of divination and design. This combined effort has taken over two years of research to accomplish. The magnificent art of Peter Paul is remarkable to say the least! Peter Paul is the youngest of my talented children and how very proud I am of each of their individual accomplishments.

It may be difficult for the reader to realize that Peter Paul is absolutely a self-taught artist. His artistic skills are so extreme from his humorous cartoons, plus his own unique paintings, and his exquisite fine art styles. When Peter Paul was about thirteen years old I told him that some day he would paint my Tarot images—and he has. It is with love and admiration that I acknowledge Peter Paul Connolly as my coauthor on this work.

ACKNOWLEDGMENTS

*I would like to thank all of my readers throughout the years;
I sincerely appreciate your interest and hope that you will enjoy
the Feng Shui Tarot Deck as much as I have.*

— Eileen Connolly

*Thanks so much Hunter for your support, love and patience
throughout this project. Alex Wagner, thanks for helping
me pull this book together. Thanks Mom for seeding
the idea and believing it could happen.*

— Peter Paul Connolly

TAROT IS A VEHICLE

Tarot is a vehicle—the experience is surprisingly similar to taking on ownership of a new car. Here we have the Feng Shui Tarot Deck: a totally innovative new concept of Tarotology guaranteed to make your journey on the "Royal Road" smooth and exhilarating. As you begin to experiment and try all the components, you may first want to get the right measure of comfort...beginning with your new Feng Shui Tarot Handbook.

SEASONING YOUR DECK

After opening the cellophane-wrapped deck, take a moment to look at the breathtaking art of Peter Paul Connolly. When you have satisfied your senses, this would be a perfect time to sit down and begin to handle the cards. Over the next several days, whenever you have a free moment—pick up your deck and enjoy how the cards look and how they feel.

When your Tarot deck is new the cards feel much different from a deck that has been "seasoned." A good way to begin the seasoning process is to begin slipping the new cards gently and randomly back into the deck. Do this as often as it feels right. I suggest you avoid shuffling the cards harshly in a "Las Vegas" style. When you feel that the cards are thoroughly intermixed, place any remaining cards back into the deck and finish with a gentle shuffle. There is no reason to deliberately invert a card, that is to say "to purposefully reverse a card." As you go through this process, some part of you, usually referred to as the "Higher Self," is busy preparing your cards so there is no need to overly concentrate at this time. Try not to be concerned, however, if you see that some cards are falling into reversed positions. Just let them fall naturally into any position. By doing so you are correctly "seasoning" your new Tarot deck.

Your next question might be...How do I know when the deck is seasoned? As you continue to handle or season the deck, your cards will begin to feel different. This unusual phenomenon is an exciting step and indicates that you have successfully impregnated your Tarot cards with your personal vibrations.

At first, the deck feels like any other deck of cards. It is only with this initial handling that you begin to feel your own energy penetrating and becoming part of your own personal Tarot deck. From the moment you begin to handle the cards, you become the new owner.

Now you may be wondering...what is the next step? As the "new owner" of this beautiful Tarot deck you have looked at the images, you have seasoned the cards. Now you would like to understand what it all means. Well, you have come to the right place. The next step is to get a basic understanding of what the Tarot deck is all about.

Keep in mind that as you explore and handle the cards you are also continuing to align and infuse the deck with your personal energy. The more you do this, the more familiar you will become with your cards. This same energy will also help you to understand your readings when you are ready to make a spread.

MAKING A SPREAD

A spread is a particular formation of Tarot cards, which are spread out in a definite order and sequence. Each card in the spread—be it major or minor—is relevant! Otherwise there would be no point in it being considered as a part of the spread or reading. The challenge and satisfaction derived from being able to decipher or interpret a spread is dependent upon your skill and patience to understand the Tarot deck. Having said that, in no way do I mean to suggest that learning about your Tarot cards is an overwhelming or intimidating task. (It is not!) It can be both fun and exhilarating. There are many different spreads that can be used. The oldest and most popular being the Celtic Cross Spread which is included in the Appendix of this handbook.

The nature of your question or inquiry determines which type of spread to choose. If you think of a spread as being a "recipe" you will realize that each spread is formatted to accommodate a particular type of question or need. You will find quite a large selection of spreads from two of my books: *Tarot, the Handbook for the Journeyman* and *Tarot, a New Handbook for the Apprentice*.

Many people want to know if it is necessary to get into the history of Tarot before learning how to use the cards.

You, yourself, are eager to see if Tarot works for you and whether it is necessary to delve into the origins and history of Tarot. Attempting to do this at the early stage of trying to learn Tarot is somewhat intimidating to say the least. Yet if you really become an avid user of your cards, it won't be too long before you start wanting to know more!

Many authors and teachers have produced excellent works for the student interested in these areas. Your personal interest will also grow as you become more attached to the Tarot. Whether it is because you enjoy collecting the many beautiful decks available, or from the natural incentive to discover the right teacher for you–that is the exciting adventure of the "Royal Road of Tarot."

WHY ARE THERE SO MANY DIFFERENT TAROT DECKS?

A good question! Each of the Tarot decks is considered to be influenced by the source and principles of the particular knowledge from which it is derived.

There are many variations in design and all of them represent the same principle and rudiments of Tarot. This in itself initiates and encourages the original interest of Tarot and what the practice of Tarotology has to offer. First we are attracted to the picture itself and how the artistic image affects us personally. Each artist has given or portrayed his or her own interpretation of the spiritual force that energizes the Tarot.

From the image or picture we see through the eye of the artist, our individual journey on the Royal Road. It is enhanced with the selection of symbols used. Each Tarot deck has come from, and embraces other aspects of, the metaphysical sciences. Ancient roots coalesce and offer a personal guidance and direction to the mystery of the higher levels of consciousness. This further initiates and encourages the original interest of Tarot and what the practice of Tarotology has to offer.

We are attracted to color, visual impression, the images and whether or not we feel comfortable with what we see or feel. Your individual sensitivity plays a great part in selecting which Tarot deck resonates with you. If you happen to be a collector of Tarot decks, your choices are not only many, but exciting as well.

GETTING STARTED

We will now prepare you for your journey of owning and using your Tarot deck. Learning Tarot, like any other method of learning, can be a stimulating new project. You begin with the deck and take the time to browse and "handle" your cards. If you are using a new Tarot deck this can be most exciting. It is my hope that as you look through the cards you are also enjoying and appreciating the pleasure they give.

Handle your new cards as much as you can even though you may not fully understand what they mean or represent at this time. Just the mere handling of the cards transfers your personal energy and the deck becomes "yours." The more you use the cards, the more familiar they become. Think of it this way; as you touch and handle the cards you are in fact transmitting the images and wisdom to some part of your Higher Consciousness so that the actual "learning" process of Tarotology will become easier and more fluid.

You will see that I used the terms "seasoning the deck" earlier in this book. The seasoning occurs immediately when you begin to handle or work with the cards. The seasoning of a new Tarot deck is of course not limited to any one particular deck. As a matter of fact I would recommend the same procedure with any new Tarot deck you purchase. The terminology that I use is what I have formulated throughout all of my books to help the Tarotologist establish his or her own level and personal connection with the Tarot deck.

Make yourself comfortable, relax, and enjoy working with your Tarot cards. Tune into the feel of the deck—the colors and images all mingling together as you begin to shuffle. Your senses will become heightened as the shuffled cards, slipping into each other, form a mystical pattern of anticipation. Be aware that your hands and fingers are responding to the hidden direction of the Higher Self. Somehow you know when the cards are ready—it's a feeling, a knowing.

An incredible process is taking place. Your vibratory flow begins to expand and melds easily to reach this unknown source. As you start to read the spread, you become attuned to your own level of sensitivity. The mind opens and your comprehensive skill begins to absorb the structure of your spread. Enjoy and create an atmosphere that is conducive to you, be it in the living room, office or a special area. Your Tarot cards make a good companion on the Royal Road of life!

FORECAST, PROGNOSIS, DIVINATION, PROPHECY

Take your time, and keep in mind that elasticity of interpretation for self or others is entirely dependent on the comprehension or lack of comprehension of the reader. Even then, one should always allow for the constant and sudden changes that alter the course and fluidity of life in general.

The more you learn about Tarot, the more you learn that it is nearly impossible to make hard fast predictions due to the many choices we have. Once a choice has been made, inevitably another choice has to be made. Often a querent who has a predicament feels devoid of any choice. Any help that you may give should be along the lines of opening the querent's thoughts toward new alternatives, new possibilities, and remembering that prevention is better than cure.

You could think of Tarotology as a form of self-therapy. By that I mean, as you learn Tarot you are also learning about life! Consider, if you will, the responsibility of being a Tarotologist and all that it incurs. Any way that you look at it, when one elects to read the cards for another person it should be done with an ethical approach and intent.

Use good common sense and be willing to listen. You could consider the wisdom contained in the spread as a framework to work within. Steer away from exaggeration and supposition. Let the Tarot unfold the pages of life and give you a deeper understanding and insight. Tarot can be enjoyable as well as informative. You certainly don't gain anything if the querent is afraid, so you can see how advisable it is to have a positive attitude. Review all of the possibilities that could help the client in the given situation. Enthusiasm can be contagious. Be a good listener and give empathy where needed. Life is surely an adventure—share this adventure with the client. The purpose of reading the Tarot is to understand the wisdom contained and to also embrace the philosophical aspect. To attempt more could very well change the whole content of the reading.

Following is a list of six items that I feel will enhance your experience with the Tarot:

1. Your Tarot Deck   4. Tarot Cover
2. Silk Scarf   5. Wooden Table
3. Wooden Box   6. Record Book

1. YOUR TAROT DECK

We have already discussed the need for you to season your cards, especially if you are working from a new deck. It is a good feeling to know that you have prepped your cards and that you are now getting ready to use them.

You may not want to discard the original box that the cards come in. If you collect Tarot decks you could keep the original box to help display your collection, keep it for sentimental reasons, or for whatever reason you feel is necessary.

2. SILK SCARF

Nothing enhances your deck more than the natural fibers of silk. Be it a piece of silk or a silk scarf. My Connolly Tarot Deck is kept in a purple silk bag, which, in turn, I keep in a wooden box. My Feng Shui Tarot Deck is kept in a gold silk bag, which is also kept in a wooden box.

I strongly feel that wrapping your deck in the protection of silk improves the vibratory tone of your cards, making the deck more conducive to accurate divination.

3. WOODEN BOX

The vibrations from natural wood are so very complementary for your Tarot deck. The cards become insulated from any possible outside influences. Whether going to the gym or the office you can feel assured that your deck is not exposed to any possible influence other than your own.

The wooden box could be a gift from someone special or an old box that you have had for a long time (just waiting for your Tarot deck)! You could also treat yourself to a wooden box, purchased especially to hold your cards. Either way, you will certainly feel a level of satisfaction once you have housed your deck in a way that pleases you.

4. TAROT COVER

Your Tarot cover should be preferably silk and large enough for you to lay out a spread; at least two feet square. If you are away from home, traveling or in unfamiliar surroundings the silk cover will prevent your Tarot deck from absorbing any distracting influences.

The colors gold, purple or royal blue provide a perfect platform or base to create a spread. These same colors are also ideal for wrapping your cards before placing the deck into the wooden box.

5. WOODEN TABLE

A wooden table is most desirable to a Tarotologist. It is excellent for laying out the cards because it greatly improves your receptivity when reading a spread. You will be amazed how the natural vibrations of wood can increase your awareness and help you to "tune into" the Higher Self.

To complete your most desired setting for Tarot, purchase or pick fresh flowers to place in a vase upon your wooden table. Whether you choose a single flower or a full bouquet of a variety of your favorite flowers, they will not only add to the overall ambience but will also encourage your focus when delineating the cards. The positive energy will also extend when you have fresh flowers in the room.

6. DAILY RECORD BOOK

You will not always understand the information you receive in a spread. This is something that all Tarotologists experience. I recommend recording your readings in a Daily Record Book so that you may reflect on them. It is not unusual to look back at your Daily Record Book and realize how accurate a previous reading really was. Sample Daily Record pages are located in the Appendix.

Keep in mind that if you consult the cards daily, the impact will not be as significant as a weekly or monthly reading. The Daily

Record Sheets can be used for weekly and monthly readings as well. Keep your sheets in a three-ring binder for easy reference.

THE TAROT DECK

The Tarot deck is really two decks combined. These two decks are known as the Major Arcana and the Minor Arcana. The Major Arcana is comprised of 22 cards. The Minor Arcana is comprised of 56 cards. Thus, the total number of cards in a Tarot Deck equals 78 cards.

MAJOR ARCANA CARDS

The Major Arcana has a total of twenty-two cards. It begins with THE FOOL, which is zero and has no number.

0 THE FOOL
1 THE MAGICIAN
2 THE HIGH PRIESTESS
3 THE EMPRESS
4 THE EMPEROR
5 THE HIEROPHANT
6 THE LOVERS
7 THE CHARIOT
8 STRENGTH

9 THE HERMIT
10 WHEEL OF FORTUNE
11 JUSTICE
12 THE HANGED MAN
13 TRANSITION
14 TEMPERANCE
15 MATERIALISM
16 THE TOWER
17 THE STAR

18 THE MOON
19 THE SUN
20 JUDGMENT
21 THE WORLD

MINOR ARCANA CARDS

The Minor Arcana is comprised of four suits; cups, swords, wands, and pentacles. The four suits in the Feng Shui Tarot Deck are represented as:

```
RED PHEONIX .......... Cups ............. SOUTH
WHITE TIGER .......... Swords .......... WEST
BLACK TORTOISE ....... Wands........... NORTH
GREEN DRAGON........ Pentacles......... EAST
```

The Minor Arcana has a total of fifty-six cards, which is divided again into two groups; the numbered cards and the court cards.

There are forty numbered cards; ace (1) through ten in each of the four suits. There are also four court cards in each suit. The court cards correspond with each of the four suits. There is a total of sixteen court cards in a Tarot deck, as follows.

Red Phoenix KING	White Tiger KING
Red Phoenix QUEEN	White Tiger QUEEN
Red Phoenix KNIGHT	White Tiger KNIGHT
Red Phoenix PAGE	White Tiger PAGE
Black Tortoise KING	Green Dragon KING
Black Tortoise QUEEN	Green Dragon QUEEN
Black Tortoise KNIGHT	Green Dragon KNIGHT
Black Tortoise PAGE	Green Dragon PAGE

APPEARANCE OF SUITS IN A SPREAD

Red Phoenix (cups)

Multiple Red Phoenixes in a spread relates to loved ones, and concerns of love.

White Tiger (swords)	Multiple White Tigers in a spread indicates emotional concerns, pressure, and effort.
Black Tortoise (wands)	Multiple Black Tortoises indicate changing vibrations, activities and movement.
Green Dragon (pentacles)	Multiple Green Dragons in a spread indicate monetary transactions, loans, banking, and other financial situations.

THE DOMINANT SUIT FACTOR

A Dominant Suit Factor occurs when you have more cards of a particular suit than others in a spread. The Dominant Suit Factor can affect any spread that you have selected for the reading.

The nature of the spread will reflect this governing aspect in a reading. When you first analyze the spread look at any Dominant Suit Factor, which, in turn, will be indicative of the focus or intent of the reading.

CLEARING AND SOLIDIFYING THE DECK

I have included a couple of procedures you may find helpful or useful when you work with the cards. If you are a stickler for doing things in a particular order then you might find that "clearing" the deck and the following "solidification" practice might be additional tools for you.

I have modified these procedures, which are very simple, and I leave it to you, the reader, as to whether or not you find them helpful.

To clear or break the deck, shuffle the cards to erase a previous spread. Do likewise if there has been prior handling of the cards.

- After the deck has been reshuffled, cut the deck into two stacks.
- Use the left hand to make a sweeping or clearing movement to the left.
- Place the stacks back together again.
- Place the left hand on the deck once more to "solidify" the deck.
- You are now ready to hand the deck back to the client or querent.

Anytime you are interrupted or have cause to move away from the cards, solidification will help to contain the energy.

UNDERSTANDING
THE MINOR & MAJOR MENTORS

The term mentor means "wise loyal advisor, a teacher or coach." In Greek mythology Mentor was the loyal friend and advisor of Odysseus and the teacher of his son Telemachus.

In order to help you understand the symbology of the Tarot, I have prepared what I call "mentors" for each of the cards. Each card has its own set of mentors—the major and the minor mentors.

The purpose of the Tarot mentors is to bring together, in an organized way, a collection of esoteric knowledge regarding each of the seventy-eight cards contained in the Tarot deck. You will see how I have combined old traditional definitions with my own method of interpretation.

Each Mentor contains the following types of information:

THE MENTOR LEGEND

- Core Aspect
- Reversed Core Aspect
- Contemplation
- Reversed Contemplation
- Directive
- Reversed Directives
- Thought Trend (Major Arcana only)
- Proximity (All Court Cards and Minor Arcana Cards)

CORE ASPECT

The Core Aspect is used when a card is in the upright position. You will note that the Core Aspect gives a general feeling of the card. Like all the cards in the deck, the emphasis is often determined by the location of the card within the spread. An example might be if a situation has already occurred, is ongoing, or if it has yet to be experienced.

REVERSED CORE ASPECT

The Reversed Core Aspect is used when a card has been placed in a reversed position. (Often referred to as being upside down). You will see that the interpretation is different—either enhanced or diminished— but not necessarily negative.

CONTEMPLATION AND REVERSED CONTEMPLATION

The Contemplation for Upright and Reversed is a simple rhyming verse. I wrote each of the rhymes to give you a sense of the Core Aspect and the Reversed Core Aspect. Some may find it easier to memorize the verse in cooperation with the Core and Reversed Aspects. The idea here is to "hit the nail on the head" to help the reader get right to the core of the situation at hand.

DIRECTIVE AND REVERSED DIRECTIVES

Both of the Directives are intended to add more depth and give a fuller or extended explanation of what is happening. The Directives also touch upon how the querent feels in the given situation. You will also see how "you" the reader can help guide the querent to better understand the circumstances involved.

THOUGHT TREND
(MAJOR ARCANA ONLY)

The Thought Trend is intended to help probe further into the information that is delineated from any Major Arcana card in the spread. The impact of a Major Arcana card can often be better understood with the help of the Thought Trend.

PROXIMITY (ALL COURT CARDS
AND MINOR ARCANA CARDS)

The court cards, along with the Minor Arcana cards, have a Proximity section. If, in your spread, you have the two selected cards (located in this Proximity section) you then have access to additional information. This additional information adds emphasis for your particular spread. These "two cards" can be located in any position within the ten-card Celtic Cross Spread.

THE MAJOR ARCANA

To refresh your memory from the earlier introduction to the deck, you know that the Tarot deck has a total of seventy-eight cards. The cards are divided into two sections, the Major and Minor Arcanas.

The twenty-two cards that comprise the Major Arcana are also known collectively as the Royal Road. When a Major Arcana card is located in the spread it immediately attracts our attention. Instantly we know that the wisdom and information gleaned has a higher degree of intensity. That being so, our attention shifts to the surrounding cards in the spread to see what mundane situation has prompted the apparent need for the additional emphasis of the major card portrayed in the spread.

The minor cards accommodate the everyday happenings; feelings, emotions, plus the need for continual decision-making. All of which add to the ups and downs of living. When we consider all the people we know—family, friends, and working relationships—we are not always sure who will do what, in any given situation. The minor cards stress or highlight how we react to the daily challenges and how we strive to reach a personal level of joy and achievement.

We are constantly aware of the silent discomforts we experience. How we feel at any given time is always relevant. So much so, that our lives are colored by these varying levels of emotion. We have learned so well to disguise our true feelings. Perhaps the fact that we can use this inner control becomes a part of the facade we project daily.

The truth of who we are can be found in the symbolism of the Major Arcana. Each of the Major Arcana cards can open vast dimensions of the Higher Consciousness, which in turn, can reveal doorways to potential, purpose, and possibility not yet explored. Like an egg waiting to be cracked open! At that point you alone can decide what you will create in your life.

When it comes to cracking the egg, our choices are varied. We can choose to scramble, boil, or fry, etc. Better still we can add "pure" genius to create an original masterpiece. Like a sleeping giant, our potential waits to be awakened. Fortunately we all manage at some time to arouse this giant and what follows usually depicts an exciting episode of life served and presented as success, joy, or a desirable achievement. Try to learn and analyze the strength and knowledge contained in the Major Arcana. Some may do this with meditation; others may take a different approach. Nevertheless you can discover your own personal path and access to the hidden wisdom waiting to be discovered through the practice of Tarotology.

I have mentioned the additional emphasis that the Major Arcana gives to a reading. The number of major cards in the spread obviously determines the importance of the delineation or information you receive. With each major card I have given you two key words to help you get a better understanding of the spread. If we look at The Fool card for example, we see the words "choice" and "focus." These two key words provide an anchor to what the spread has to reveal as a whole.

Following the two key words, I have given you some further insight to help you expand your thoughts and connect these thoughts to the rest of the spread. Continuity of thought and focus is essential to comprehend the wisdom that the spread portrays in its entirety.

THE FOOL – CHOICE & FOCUS

When you begin to contemplate The Fool card you are well aware that you have wiped the slate clean. As you prepare to make a fresh new start it is always with the last experience or lesson you have undergone in mind. It is with every good intent that you consider the next step. Making this first choice will determine and color the eventual outcome.

THE MAGICIAN – INDIVIDUALITY & CREATIVITY

The time for action and decision is now yours. You realize that you are being observed and that your sense of individuality must not be considered as an imposition to those around you. At the same time you realize how important it is to be your own person. Retaining a new kind of balance strengthens your goals and helps you to make them happen.

THE HIGH PRIESTESS – INTUITION & COOPERATION

Your sensitivity urges you to listen to how others may feel. Ideas and plans you have not yet shared or discussed are now developing. There are two possibilities that you need to consider, especially before you move further and make a commitment. Weigh the whole situation carefully. There is still something missing! Be patient, the missing "piece" will soon fall into place.

THE EMPRESS — ABUNDANCE & PROSPERITY

This feeling of inner contentment and having it all together is the beginning of a new prosperity. You now feel that you have something worthwhile to build upon. This root base is both solid and firm. This growth cycle will help you to realize what it has taken to reach this level. Enjoy the security you have earned. Your achievement will open many doors of opportunity. Don't be afraid to enjoy!

THE EMPEROR — DISCIPLINE & FOUNDATIONS

Continue to build a firm base before going further. Refuse to get embroiled in other people's ideas. Actually, you are right where you need to be—focused on what you want to accomplish. Any further diversion away from your original goal will only prove to be another setback. This is it! Get on the ball and you will achieve results.

THE HIEROPHANT — FREEDOM & CROSSROADS

You have been getting the feeling that you are not going anywhere—fast. It might appear to you that every time you get to this step you are either blocked or there is always something to prevent you from getting what you need. Take a moment and review past patterns. Conforming to what others expect of you could appear to be the reason. Do your own thing, be your own person, and the restrictions will melt away.

THE LOVERS — HIGHER CHOICE & DECISIONS

It is not always easy to change how things are. But you know that some changes have to be made by you (or by someone close to you). The difficulty is not in making the decision but in arriving at an agreeable or satisfactory solution. Two heads are better than one. It is better to be open, not on the defensive. Trying to do this on your own is not the answer. Seek guidance from a trusted loved one.

THE CHARIOT — CONTROL & PROGRESS

At last, you seem to be sloughing off the residue of old emotional hang-ups. It would be so easy just to slip back into the old stuff, but the strength of The Chariot is strong enough to pull you forward and away toward a fresh new start. Progress is ahead and all you have to do is sit in the driver's seat.

STRENGTH — LOVE & PATIENCE

Do not allow what comes next to alter your outlook or approach. You are in a good position to see and enjoy the future results of your endeavors. Try not to be impatient, as this would just take you off course. Do what you have to do to give assurance. You have written the script, now get ready to enjoy the play! Keep in mind that you are ahead of the game and your patience will be tested.

THE HERMIT — WISDOM & COMMON SENSE

The secret here is to recognize that you are avoiding the next step. Dancing around the issue will eventually make you "A day late and a dollar short." The next step you are avoiding is the next step—you must move forward. You are so close to bringing it all together. Believe in yourself, you can do it! No one else can come up with a better way or better answer. You know what to do from here, use your good common sense.

WHEEL OF FORTUNE   CHANGE & ADAPTATION

The Wheel of Life is in continual motion. After what seems to be a lull with all the complexities of delay and the accompanying frustrations, your personal wheel is now beginning to move in an upward trend. With this shifting, the "flood gates open" and you are back in action again! As the pressures start to ease off, be more flexible, less uptight, and adapt accordingly.

JUSTICE — BALANCE & KARMA

Now you may begin to put the past behind you. In letting go, you are free to get that sense of personal order back where it should be. All things considered, it is best to leave well enough alone and call it a day. This gives you the ability to take advantage of an unusual karmic opportunity. It is one of those times that you will land on your feet. As long as you feel good about what you do next, then you will not feel that you are creating a new karmic situation.

THE HANGED MAN — CONTEMPLATION & ANTICIPATION

You have done well to hold off! Your ability to visualize what you want is soon to become a reality. Continue in the same way, keeping your ideas/plans intact. The last hurdle is in view and it's just a matter of how others respond. Your reaction will be that of strong confidence and your ability to finish what you started. Changes are bound to occur, so keep cool. Whatever you do, don't allow your feathers to get ruffled!

TRANSITION — TOTAL CHANGE & NEW BEGINNINGS

Take another look at this stunning card. You have now begun to emerge, the new image is so unlike the "old you." This is an exciting transformation! All that has happened to cause this change is now becoming the "new you." Although the transparency still retains the shadow of your former self, you have successfully proven that you are now well on the way to a new mastery of self.

TEMPERANCE — EQUATION & HARMONY

The emphasis here is on balance. In the rush to accomplish, you can lose sight of your objective. Looking at the Temperance card I am reminded of the old saying, "Many a slip twixt cup and lip." Enjoy the feeling of harmony as you observe the coming together of your well-grounded plans. Maintain the balance you have created and your gift of patience will be rewarded twofold.

MATERIALISM — INDULGENCE & DISCONTENTMENT

It has become important to reevaluate the present circumstances. Put your pride and personal interests on one side and really take a long look. One thing is certain; it is not wise to prolong this situation. Clinging to what you don't have is ludicrous, wanting more is even worse! Something has to give; otherwise the pressure you feel will escalate beyond sense and reason. Review the whole situation and begin to make reparable solutions where needed.

THE TOWER — RELEASE & BREAKDOWN

A flood of insecurity saturates the equilibrium. You are experiencing the release of old negativity. Keep in mind that the karmic impact is essentially a clearing process that takes you away from all that is not conducive to your needs. This release and breakdown may affect different areas in life that are in need of clearance. Allow this process to happen so that you can accept new opportunities in a bright new future.

THE STAR — HEALING & INSPIRATION

The tranquility of The Star not only surpasses but also helps to overcome bruised relationships, a business collapse, or any major disappointment. This beautiful symbol strongly indicates that you are now to that point—the threshold—of where you will experience a transformation. The Star is now shining for you and it will shed its light on accomplishment, inspiration, healing, and prosperity.

THE MOON — SENSITIVITY & FAITH

Your sensitivity comes to the forefront. These feelings have gradually developed and you find that you are more receptive to what is happening around you. The change has been subtle and you are discovering a new dimension of thought and possibility. As you learn to trust and expand your sensitivity, know that it can serve you well and give you a new sense of independence. Your consciousness is preparing to enter this portal.

THE SUN — ATTAINMENT & SUCCESS

Attainment and success come in many shapes and sizes. When The Sun is in the spread, you will know that opportunity is well on the way. If The Sun is in the tenth Celtic Cross Spread position, the answer to a question is "Yes"! Any doubt regarding hopes and desires begin to dissipate when The Sun impregnates the spread. The message of joy and prosperity has officially begun. As you delineate the spread, look for a pattern of joy in the making.

JUDGMENT — RENEWAL & POSITIVE KARMA

It may have been quite some time since you felt this way. Life has taken a unique turn for the better. Wonderful changes are starting to happen. Don't hesitate to be "yourself." It is an excellent time to cut the strings of unwanted ties. Some part of you feels the new energy pouring in. It appears as though the world is opening doors for you. As you get more into the feel of this cycle, do not hesitate to be your own person!

THE WORLD — FREEDOM & RELEASE

The word change is at the top your "Life Menu." You are ready to make several changes, one of which could be in relation to career and/or residence. Success highlights your current status. Restrictions are peeling away, leaving you free to pursue your intent. You could be feeling that if you blinked your eyes it would all go away. Feel confident that you are supported firmly by those around you, and you can trust that what is to come will be very real.

VERIFICATION CARDS

A Tarot deck may be considered an oracle. It contains a specific number of cards including the Major and Minor Arcanas, which gives a total number of seventy-eight cards in all. Included in the minor cards each suit has four court cards. In its entirety, the deck becomes the oracle. If a card is extracted then the oracle is made imperfect! Much like the alphabet; if one letter were missing, your ability to write would be inhibited because you would be unable to complete certain words. We have a similar situation with the Tarot cards. Tarot is an esoteric language and with regular use you will learn to be conversant. For example, you would soon learn that a Celtic Cross Spread is far more than ten simple statements. You can only express so much if you don't have the command of the language. To become fluent and lucid requires practice.

To ensure that the oracle remains intact, the reader determines which card or cards to select that represent the person in question. This could be the querent and/or other people involved with the querent. The card or cards selected are called Verification Cards. They remain in the deck and are read as part of the spread.

As you well know, our daily life is divided into various roles. If, for example, you are a parent and your question is regarding the family then in turn you would select Verification Cards that you feel are appropriate for each of the individual family members. On the other hand, if directing your question toward your business or job, then again you would select the most fitting Verification Card(s) to represent the people involved with regard to your question.

Therefore, it is important that before you begin the reading, you decide which of the court cards best represent the people involved. It won't take long before you develop a list of familiar names, and then when the cards you selected turn up in the reading you will have an understanding of "who is who" and how they may relate in the given situation.

It could be helpful, at least when you first start working with Verification Cards to make a note of your pre-selected cards. And don't forget to include your own Verification Cards if you play a part in the reading. If you are working with a client, it is always helpful to listen carefully and get a good sense of whom you will select for the client's Verification Cards.

Before we go further, lets have a recap here: You know that the tarot deck is an oracle. We have discussed how Verification Cards are helpful when trying to determine "who is who" in your reading. And just a reminder, the Verification Cards that you have selected must remain in the deck.

HOW COURT CARDS BECOME YOUR VERIFICATION CARDS

Court cards serve as Verification Cards because they represent people. The dual purpose of the court card as a Verification Card is not a complex situation. The apparent duality only occurs when the court card you have chosen also becomes a Verification Card. This simply means that:

1. You read the court card as you would normally read a court card.
2. You also recognize the court card as the Verification Card you selected.

3. The dual aspect allows you, the reader, to understand the Verification Card is in the spread and how the Verification Card relates to the spread or reading as a whole.
4. The card selected as a Verification Card also becomes a part of the reading and should be interpreted accordingly.
5. Initially you are using a Verification Card to represent you or the querent in the spread.
6. Verification cards are also used to represent the people you consider influential in your life.

The information found in the "mentors" that corresponds with the Verification Card you selected would provide additional insight.

THE FOUR DISTINCT COURT FAMILIES

We have in all, a total of sixteen court cards. These sixteen court cards are divided into four groups that are identified as the four suits. Each of these suits has a total of four court cards namely: King, Queen, Knight, and Page.

In the Feng Shui Tarot Deck the suits are recognized as follows:

Swords . . . . WHITE TIGER
Pentacles . . . . GREEN DRAGON
Wands. . . . . BLACK TORTOISE
Cups . . . . RED PHEONIX

THE NATURE OR THEME OF THE COURT CARDS

Primarily the court cards represent human beings. Once you realize that each set of four suits has its own nature or personality, it won't take too long to grasp the concept. If, for example, we take a look at the Green Dragon court cards you can see how each of them are related to each other.

Although each suit contains a total of four court cards, they also have their own individual nature. The Green Dragon suit, just as the other suits, extends its nature or theme throughout the suit. This provides an added emphasis to the purpose or overall meaning of each individual suit.

Once you have the understanding and feel comfortable with the purpose, feeling, or message that each of the suits conveys, you will then discover that the individual minor cards of the suits will be more readily understood.

SELECTING THE VERIFICATION CARD

This is a generalized list of categories appertaining to the four suits. From these suggested groupings you can select the appropriate Verification Card to help you focus on the reading without being overly concerned as to whether you have chosen the right Verification Card for the purpose of your Tarot spread.

WHITE TIGER (SWORDS)

The White Tiger suit deals with the following:

Concerns	Severance and separation
Pressures	Ill health
Effort	Overcoming obstacles
Legal situations	New beginnings
Responsibilities	

GREEN DRAGON (PENTACLES)

The Green Dragon suit deals with the following:

Monetary transactions	Loans
Banking	Real estate
Prosperity	Promotion
Financial obligations	Investments
Financial struggle/loss	

BLACK TORTOISE (WANDS)

The Black Tortoise suit deals with the following:

Business situations	Work or Job related
Boss and/or supervisor	Colleagues
Plans	Organizing
Projects	Home organization
Discipline	

RED PHEONIX (CUPS)

The Red Phoenix suit deals with the following:

Emotions	Love
Happiness	Personal relationships
Soul Mate	Family relationships
Children	Karmic ties
Healing	

FOCUS ON YOU

There are so many facets of YOU...A person can play so many different roles and wear so many hats, sometimes simultaneously. This can be a dilemma when it gets down to choosing a Verification Card. You are "who you are" depending on "who you are" in any given situation.

The business executive at home discards the dirty laundry, takes out the trash, and helps the kids do their homework. The writer of books, the builder of homes, the concierge at your favorite hotel, the mom at home, the taxi driver, and anyone who is out there doing what they have to do—all eventually arrive home and shift mental gears. We become another facet of who we are. It is important to really consider how we deal with this when we are working with the Tarot.

The CEO may very well be curious as to whether or not he or she should be looking at a purely domestic issue. The homemaker could be contemplating the possibility of opening a new business. So we see here that it is not who you are or any particular status that determines how you select your Verification Card.

Where are you coming from and what is your focus? That is the more relevant question.

We have arrived at a point where you now have a good idea as to how your pre-selected Verification Card can help you focus on your reading. By narrowing the margin of possibilities available, you can begin to delineate the spread with a reasonable level of confidence.

QUESTIONS FROM
MY READERS & STUDENTS

I thought you would find these frequently asked questions helpful in regard to Verification Cards.

Q: *I have two questions entirely unrelated to each other. Both are equally important to me. How do I know that the reading will address each separately?*

A: First select a Verification Card that represents you in the first particular situation. Then select Verification Cards for the people involved in this first question. After you have satisfactorily completed the first spread, you can clear the deck, then solidify it, and proceed to start fresh with a new reading. Once again, you would select a suitable or second Verification Card for you, this time focusing on the new set of circumstances presented by the second question.

Q: *I have a baby, what Verification Card do I use?*

A: Use the Page to represent your baby. This is a good question and I would like to add that it is not always easy to categorize or assess a given age especially after adolescence. A general guide would be:

KING = Mature Man
QUEEN = Mature Woman
KNIGHT = Young Man
PAGE = Young Boy or Girl

The level of maturity or lack of maturity differs according to the person. I would suggest that you use discretion and sensitivity when contemplating the Verification Card. Again, one has to consider the circumstances, as well as the approach and attitude toward the situation before allocating a Verification Card.

Q: *I have done several readings and I accommodate for my Verification Cards. Why do I get court cards in the spread, which are not my Verification Cards and who do they represent?*

A: In the First Handbook for the Master I have made reference to the "Unplaced Verification Card." When an unverified court card appears in the spread, we have the possibility of an unexpected influence coming into the querent's present affairs.
I would further add that when the Page brings the "Second Seed," (see *Handbook for the Journeyman*) we can expect to find persons appearing in the spread that are not considered to have any possible influence at this time. This would then account for any unplaced Verification Cards that represent further influences not yet known at the time of the reading.

Q: *I would like to read the Tarot about me. I have so many questions, I don't know where to begin. It is not one of those situations where I have "one" specific question. I have several—all about me.*

A: Becoming familiar with your deck and the images portrayed within it helps considerably when working with the Tarot. When reading for yourself in depth, the simplest method would be to select one of the four Kings or one of the four Queens. You can then proceed with a Celtic Cross Spread or the spread of your choice for each of the questions you may have.

HOW FENG SHUI & TAROT CONNECT

BY PETER PAUL CONNOLLY

Over the centuries the Chinese culture has developed a connection and understanding of the role unseen energies play in their everyday lives. The I-Ching, acupuncture and the martial arts are all the result of this collective cultural leaning toward the acknowledgment and belief that everything, even solid physical form, is energy. This acceptance has led to the widespread importance and reliance on such metaphysical practices as Feng Shui. The intuitive "feel" people get of a particular location the moment they encounter it is the root of Feng Shui.

Feng Shui is a method of understanding and manipulating the dynamic balance of energy or "chi" present in nature. It is an intuitive sense of the harmony and balance or obstruction and stagnation of energy in your everyday surroundings. Awareness and knowledge of Feng Shui equips people with the necessary tools to take steps in correcting imbalances or enhancing and solidifying beneficial balanced conditions in their immediate environment.

Feng Shui translates literally into "wind and water," which is suggestive of its ancient origins. It hints at the necessity to align how we conduct our lives with the forces of nature. Both air and water are the most fundamental elements of life. Wind and water by their very nature are suggestive of movement and interaction. This thought can also be applied to the dynamic force and energy of nature as a whole.

For well over two thousand years, through keen observation and recording of natural forces and phenomena, the Chinese have gradually compiled an ever-evolving system of knowledge. Its intricacies and complexities are seemingly boundless. But without compromising the integrity of Feng Shui, the basic concepts can be extracted and understood.

FORM SCHOOL
AND COMPASS SCHOOL

There are two predominant schools of thought in Feng Shui—the Form School and the Compass School. The form school is based on the influence of environmental conditions, the physical composition of one's immediate surroundings, as well as the shape, material, and color of the scenic formations of those surroundings.

Whereas, the compass school is focused primarily on direction, and is concerned with the directional orientation of a site within a particular environment. It also considers the ramifications of the unimpeded or blocked flow of "chi" depending on directional orientation. The compass school of thought developed from Feng Shui practitioners originating from the somewhat featureless, flat plains of northern China and became inextricably melded with the generally more topographic focus of the form school.

Each school or method stands on its own as a viable vehicle for ascertaining the energy flow of a given situation. However, a more complete picture is gained from the conjunction of the two methods.

Upon researching Feng Shui, it became apparent to me that different authors chose aspects of Feng Shui that struck their interest and worked for them. They focused on that particular aspect as the core of their understanding of Feng Shui. For example, I found one book on Feng Shui to be nearly entirely about water formations, whereas another book was predominantly about interiors.

The development of the different schools of Feng Shui and the diverse interpretations that have evolved over the centuries, have rendered it nearly impossible to incorporate all of these aspects of Feng Shui into a concise and useable formula to integrate with Tarot.

So I decided to condense the vast ocean of information concerning Feng Shui into something compatible and workable for my purposes. Which, in my case, is the overall feel, flow, and interplay of the physical surroundings of characters or suit animals within the confines of a tarot card. I also considered the positive, negative, or neutral effect a particular scenario may have on those characters involved.

This gives me the parameters to mold and create a situation of balance or imbalance within the boundaries of a static visual picture or painting depending on the combinations of elements present within that particular scenario.

I have found that one of the main deciding factors in focusing primarily on the form school of Feng Shui, as opposed to the compass school, is the fact that direction cannot be pleasingly implied within the context of a two dimensional image.

Utilizing and identifying with the form school enables me to delineate both aspects of Tarot and Feng Shui in a visually appealing format. This allows me to convey the intended information both clearly and concisely.

THE BAGUA

The bagua is a system or visual diagram which is used to show the connections and correlations of the various components of certain esoteric sciences. These esoteric sciences have converged and evolved over time to form the collective body of information that is Feng Shui.

The lay out of the bagua can be thought of as a compass divided into eight directions. At the center of the bagua lies the Tai Chi symbol, more commonly referred to as the Yin Yang symbol. This simple but powerful symbol represents the co-existence of opposites—the maintaining of the dynamic equilibrium present in the universe and the unbounded potentiality of the manifestation of all things.

In Feng Shui, the life affirming, auspicious southerly direction holds the esteemed position at the top of the compass. North is at the bottom. East is to the left and west is to the right.

The four cardinal points of the compass, north, south, east, and west each have a corresponding animal associated with them.

- SOUTH is represented by the RED PHOENIX, a mythical bird of great beauty, warmth, and undying inspiration.

- WEST features the WHITE TIGER, a powerful creature evoking a sense of strength, defense, and a need for control.

- The BLACK TORTOISE is the symbolic animal of the NORTH. The Black Tortoise has the enduring qualities of stability, longevity, and security.

- EAST is represented by the GREEN DRAGON that symbolizes intellect and power with a serene yet potent spiritual presence.

In the Feng Shui Tarot deck these four animals represent the four suits of the Minor Arcana. Each of these suits also has a corre-

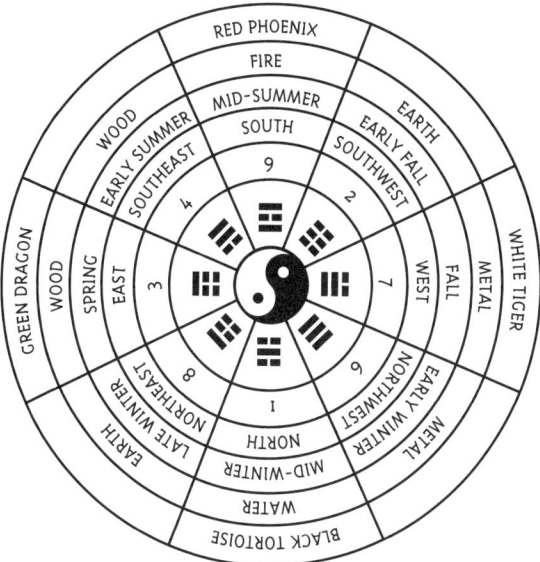

sponding season, with the remaining divisions of the bagua representing periods of mid-season.

The correlations continue with each division assigned an element and a number. The numbers follow a convoluted order as can be seen in the diagram of the bagua. The numbers one through nine, with "five" being at the center, continue with the number ten starting the sequence over in the same position as number one. Number eleven would be considered number two on the bagua, number twelve would be three, and so on.

Also, included on the bagua are "The Eight Tri Grams." Each tri gram consists of broken or unbroken lines. A combination of three of these lines comprise a single tri gram. The solid or unbroken line is considered a "Yang" line and the broken line, a "Yin" line. From these eight combinations of Yin and Yang lines, all the fundamental conditions on earth and in the cosmos are said to be represented.

The tri grams come from the I-Ching or *The Book of Changes.* This text was a vast undertaking accomplished thousands of years ago by Chinese scholars. In *The Book of Changes,* the theory of Yin and Yang was traced, through sixty-four chapters, from its conception to the eight tri grams present on the Bagua—ultimately to the point where the interaction of Yin and Yang is said to encompass all the constantly evolving phenomena we experience.

From nothing comes something. Through the balance and interplay of these opposites, the perpetual yielding force of the Yin and the ever-dominating force of the Yang are forever locked in a dance of flowing equilibrium. From this process of yielding and domination springs forth every possible interplay between give and take, dark and light, action and rest, feminine and masculine. This gives rise to the potential creation of everything in existence, or what is referred to in Taoist teachings as "The Ten Thousand Things." Interestingly, the most cutting edge theories of quantum physics seem to mirror and embrace the concept of the I-Ching.

Each of the eight tri grams also correlates with a family member. I use four of the eight tri grams to describe the family relationships of the court cards. The court "family" of each suit is the same.

- The Page is "Tui" which means "youngest daughter."
  The tri gram for The Page is ☱

- The Knight is considered the eldest son or "Chen."
  The Knight's tri gram is ☳

- The Queen is "K'un" which translates to "Mother."
  The Queen's tri gram is ☷

- The King is "Ch'ien" meaning "Father."
  The King's tri gram is ☰

THE ELEMENTAL FORMS

The physical shape of the features in a landscape, whether they are naturally formed or man-made, are categorized by the five elements: wood, fire, earth, metal, and water. An environment conducive to the flow of "chi" or an environment that obstructs the gentle meandering of positive "chi" energy can be determined by the combination and proximity of these elements.

First it is necessary to determine the dominant elements of a location made evident by their form or shape.

THE WOOD ELEMENT. Trees are vertical and tall, so environmental features of the "wood" element are depicted by structures that are columnar in shape, such as the tall cylindrical mountains of southern China. (These mountains are also prominently featured in the Green Dragon suit.) Chimneys, poles, and, of course, trees are also considered to be of the wood element.

THE FIRE ELEMENT. Flames can be described as pointed. Features of the "fire" element are also pointed, such as the jagged peaks of mountains or the sharp points of steep roofs or spires.

THE EARTH ELEMENT. Features of the "earth" element are defined by their low, flat form. A vast plain, a flat-topped building, a flat hill, or plateau are all considered to be of the earth element.

THE METAL ELEMENT. The shape of a coin is round. The "metal" element reveals itself in curved and rounded forms, such as rolling hills or domed roofs.

THE WATER ELEMENT. Water has no particular form or shape yet can assume any shape. The "water" element is suggested by irregular or nondescript hills, or oddly constructed buildings such as buildings with multiple additions of different shapes and sizes.

THE GENERATIVE & DESTRUCTIVE CYCLES

The Chinese have distilled all physical phenomena of the natural world into the five elements. The interplay of these five elements can be further divided into two major cycles of interaction; the generative cycle of elements and the destructive cycle of elements. The generative cycle of elements can be viewed as a spiraling, symbiotic cycle of balance where each element generates the next in a continually evolving sequence.

The generative cycle can be thought of like this:

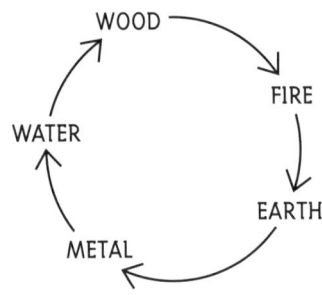

WOOD . . . . . . .Burns producing →

FIRE . . . . .Which leaves behind ash →

EARTH . . . . . . .Which is the source of →

METAL . . . . . . .Which melts into a flowing substance like →

WATER . . . . . .Which sustains the growth of →

And so on...

Alternately, the destructive cycle of elements is a cycle of imbalance. In this cycle each element tends to destroy or diminish the next one in the sequence.

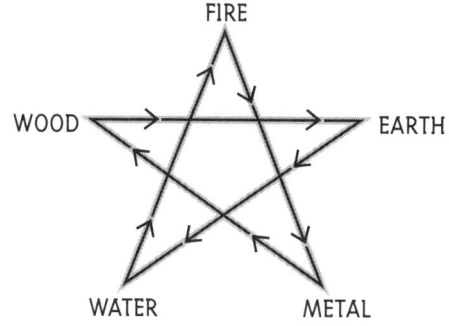

```
WOOD . . . . . . . . . . .Draws nutrients from →
EARTH . . . . . . . . . . .Which pollutes and blocks →
WATER  . . . . . . . . . .Which extinguishes →
FIRE  . . . . . . . . . . .Which melts →
METAL . . . . . . . . . . .Which chops down →
```

And so on...

SITE AND ENVIRONMENT

In the context of the Feng Shui Tarot deck, each card of the Major Arcana is assigned a dominant element determined by the number of the card. Each card of the Minor Arcana is delegated a suit element and a secondary element also determined by the number of the card. Later in this chapter I will give a full explanation of how these elements are determined. First, I want to explain the significance of the "site" and "environment" of a card and how that correlates with the interaction of the given elements.

In the Feng Shui Tarot deck, the "site" refers to the immediate area occupied by a character and/or suit animal of a particular card. It could include the building the character occupies, a small body of water the suit animal or character is standing next to, or interacting with. A site could also encompass a grove of trees, a hill-top, etc.

The "environment" of a card refers to the landscape or outlying areas that contain the site. The environment could consist of a ridge of wooded mountain peaks, an ocean, or a vast desert plain, to name a few.

I will use the White Tiger Ace (Ace of Swords) as an example to demonstrate the relationship of the site to the environment. In the White Tiger Ace, the tiger is crouched at the bank of a small still pool, drinking. In the background are rolling hills and rounded stands of trees that extend to the horizon. The sandy bank and small pool comprise the site of the card and the surrounding hills and trees define the extent of the environment. The site is considered the immediate surroundings and the environment is the visible landscape which houses or contains the site.

DETERMINING SITE AND ENVIRONMENT OF A CARD

On the bagua, there is a division of space for every number, one through nine. When number ten is reached, the sequence starts over again at number one. (Number ten falling in the same position as the number one.)

In the Major Arcana there are twenty-two numbered cards starting with zero, which is The Fool, and ending with number twenty-one, The World. Since The Fool is numbered zero, on the bagua the number before one would be number nine. (Since the cycle of one through nine is repeated indefinitely.)

Therefore, The Fool coincides with the number nine on the bagua. The second card is The Magician, which is number one in the Major Arcana, and also number one on the bagua, and so on.

On the bagua each number also corresponds with an element. In the Major Arcana this element then becomes the assigned element of either the site or the environment of that particular card. The meaning of the card depends on if the assigned element becomes the "site" element or the element of the "environment."

In the Minor Arcana, the animal that is representative of a particular suit determines the environmental element of every card in that suit. Each of the four suit animals is associated with a direction and an element of the bagua.

Red Phoenix	Fire	(South)
White Tiger	Metal	(West)
Black Tortoise	Water	(North)
Green Dragon	Wood	(East)

For example, the environment of every card in the Green Dragon (Pentacles) suit is wood, and the environment of every card in the Black Tortoise (Wands) suit is water, etc.

The numbered cards of the Minor Arcana are the Ace (one) through ten of each suit. The site of every numbered card in the Minor Arcana is determined by the number of that card corresponding to a particular element on the bagua.

Since the court cards are not numbered, the site of the court cards from each suit is determined by the correlation of the given familial relationship with its corresponding tri gram on the bagua. And that tri gram also connects with a certain element.

Page	=	Youngest Daughter	"Tui"		= Metal
Knight	=	Eldest Son	"Chen"		= Wood
Queen	=	Mother	"K'Un"		= Earth
King	=	Father	"Ch'Ien"		= Metal

I'll use the Black Tortoise III as an example of how the site and environment of a particular card is determined.

Because the environment of every card in the Black Tortoise suit is the element water, naturally the environmental element of the Black Tortoise III card is also water.

The site of the Black Tortoise III is the element wood because the number three corresponds with the element wood on the bagua.

So, from this information we have determined that the Black Tortoise III card has a wood site within a water environment.

Next, I will explain what these combinations of elements indicate and how the meanings of the cards are defined and manipulated by the introduction of controlling elements.

CONTROLLING ELEMENTS

In the Feng Shui Tarot Deck, controlling elements are employed to remedy the imbalance of unharmonious combinations of elements. But depending on the meaning of the card, an element may also be introduced to throw the balance of a harmonious combination of elements off kilter.

Examples of such controlling elements are defined in the following four scenarios:

If the given combination of a site and environmental elements fall in the generative order of elements, and the overall meaning of the card is positive, then the use of controlling elements are not necessary. An example of this scenario would be the Black Tortoise IV on page 174.

If the given combination of elements are in the generative cycle of elements, but the meaning of the card is generally negative, then an element is introduced as a means to cause discord or imbalance denoting the negative connotation of that card. An example of this scenario would be the White Tiger VII on page 124.

If the given combination of elements are in the destructive cycle of elements and the card has a positive meaning, then a controlling element is introduced to balance the situation, reflecting the harmony inherent in the card. An example of this scenario would be the Green Dragon VIII on page 154.

If the given combination of elements are in the destructive cycle of elements and the meaning of the card is somewhat negative, then the natural imbalance of the card is already defined without the introduction of an additional element. An example of this scenario would be the Materialism on page 90.

In the actual practice of Feng Shui, as in the Feng Shui Tarot Deck, how a controlling element is implemented is quite open ended. As mentioned earlier, there are many physical and representational manifestations of each element and any facet or aspect of a given element can be used to define the presence of that element.

For example, if a wood site is under threat from a metal environment, then the fire element can be introduced as a controlling element by virtue of the fact that it destroys or diminishes the threatening element.

Visually depicting the fire element can be done in many ways. I could create a ridge of pointed mountain peaks and utilize the color red in some fashion, or introduce the presence of livestock, since, in Feng Shui, the color of blood represents the fire element. Therefore, animals, or materials derived from animals, are considered to be of the fire element.

The element wood can be depicted by the presence of trees, a wooden gate, a symbol of the green dragon, or a tall, soaring, columnar shaped mountain. The same can be said of the remaining elements.

I will use the White Tiger III as an example of how a controlling element is implemented and how the site, environment and controlling elements are visually composed to create a scene in which a character reacts to imply the meaning of the card.

WHITE TIGER III

Number three on the bagua corresponds to the element wood. The wood site is delineated by the tall, narrow pagoda tower on the right. In this case, the wood element is being represented by its elemental form rather than the material of which it consists. In this setting, the metal environment threatens the wood site. Metal dominates or chops down wood in the destructive cycle of elements. This discord has been remedied by the introduction of the water element in the form of a small pond.

The nourishing energy of water generates the element under threat, in this case the wood element, thereby establishing a dynamic balance.

A ravine separates the tiger from this balanced scenario. This division symbolizes the emotional stress, upheaval, and loneliness caused by severance.

I have described in this chapter the method or formula used to depict the basic principles of form school Feng Shui in a clear, concise, and visually appealing manner. And in conjunction with the backdrop of either balanced or imbalanced Feng Shui landscapes, I have implied the meanings of the Tarot cards through the character or suit animal's interaction with their surroundings.

As I mentioned earlier, I feel as if all esoteric sciences are borne of the same inexplicable spiritual inspiration or experience that everyone attempts to describe through the limited use of language. Taking this into consideration, the seemingly unlikely paring of Tarot and Feng Shui no longer seems so strange.

THE FENG SHUI TAROT DECK

In this section of the Feng Shui Tarot Handbook, each card is described in depth. Both the Feng Shui descriptions and the Tarot aspects of each card are broken down in a concise and accessible manner for easy reference.

THE MAJOR MENTORS
THE MAJOR ARCANA

0 ....The Fool	XI ....Justice
I ....The Magician	XII........The Hanged Man
II..........The High Priestess	XIII ......The Transition
III ....The Empress	XIV ......Temperance
IV ....The Emperor	XV ......Materialism
V ....The Hierophant	XVI ......The Tower
VI ....The Lovers	XVII......The Star
VII........The Chariot	XVIII ....The Moon
VIII ......Strength	XIX ......The Sun
IX ....The Hermit	XX........Judgment
X ....Wheel of Fortune	XXI ......The World

0—THE FOOL—FENG SHUI

DOMINANT ELEMENT: Fire
TRI GRAM: ☲
DIRECTION: South

The Fool, portrayed as a female, has arrived at a crossroads. Having laid down her walking stick, she observes how the snake has rapidly coiled itself around the stick on the ground. The thoughts and opinions of mankind are represented by the snake. The snake is attempting to coerce The Fool to choose the direction that leads back toward the water. The water site, represented by the waves lapping the shore, is within a fire environment. This fire environment is depicted by the sun and the jagged mountain peaks. Fire follows water in the destructive cycle of elements. Due to this situation, palm trees (wood element) have been added to enhance the fire environment. This balanced scenario encourages The Fool to make the choice that is right for herself, the true choice, not the choice motivated by other's opinions. One can also see that The Fool has her finger pointing to the "Li" symbol on her belt, meaning middle daughter, which also falls under the fire element in the sequence of the Bagua. This further enhances the balance and establishes The Fool's own identity.

0 —THE FOOL —TAROT

CORE ASPECT: The Fool presents a Major Choice on your Life path. The decision to make this choice should not be taken lightly. Consider how you reached this crossroad. What are the consequences? Does it change or improve your present status? If you consider the choice to be beneficial, then you will experience the joy and satisfaction of having made a wise choice.

REVERSED CORE ASPECT: Conflicting opinions only prove to confuse you. Take time out to contemplate what is taking place. Review past endeavors and try to determine if you are happy with the results. If you feel overwhelmed and unable to produce in the way you had originally envisioned, then it's time to discover why.

CONTEMPLATION: Power of choice before you now. It must be done, consider how.

REVERSED CONTEMPLATION: Discontent, heave a sigh, review the past, discover why.

DIRECTIVE: In the process of arriving at a decision, before coming to a conclusion be absolutely sure that it is your decision! Clarify the whole issue. The Fool presents a major choice and it has to be yours or you will not be happy with the results. Consider all aspects and then you can go forward.

REVERSED DIRECTIVE: Listen to your Higher Self. Are you content with the way things are? Consider the alternative and also the consequences. A need to clarify. Prevent misunderstanding before the situation deteriorates further.

THOUGHT TREND: Each day is a new beginning. Try to leave yesterday alone. See today as a new opportunity and set a new pattern of thought and action. Disentangle the old coils of concern. Begin new endeavors. Create the new you and plant new seeds as you make new choices.

1—THE MAGICIAN—FENG SHUI

DOMINANT ELEMENT: Water

TRI GRAM: ☵

DIRECTION: North

The Magician has, at his command, all four animals of the four cardinal compass points, each of which correlates to subsequent Tarot suits. The Magician is the first numbered card. On the Bagua, the element associated with number one is water. Therefore, The Magician's environment is water, depicted here by the snow, clouds, and irregular shape of the rock formations. The Magician's water site being the same element as his environment allows him ultimate creativity and fluidity in forging his life path. On The Magician's coat are clouds and water representing Feng Shui, which translates literally to wind and water.

1—THE MAGICIAN—TAROT

CORE ASPECT: The strength and power of the Magician can motivate all seeds of possibility. You already have the embryo of what you want. You have recently taken a step further toward your intent. Time is of the essence—act now. Procrastination could delay the anticipated results. Let your creative juices flow and act upon what you feel. Put a sense of order and determination into your plan and make your plan work.

REVERSED CORE ASPECT: Consider whom you are leaning on and why. You need a different outlook on life. Perhaps you should consider how you misuse your talents. Meet obstacles full on. Analyze your approach and think how it may affect those around you. Sometimes the easy way proves to be the long way. Deeper insight could show you what is actually taking place.

CONTEMPLATION: Use this strength and now create. Acting now will stop the wait.

REVERSED CONTEMPLATION: Review the past, make a new start, feel the hope within your heart.

DIRECTIVE: You are on the right track! Early signs of new possibilities. As you go in this new direction keep focused on your goal. Cycle of success is now beginning.

REVERSED DIRECTIVE: A change in attitude could be the answer. Insecurity leads you to doubt. Check the whole scenario, see how you stand and then you can make new decisions.

THOUGHT TREND: It's an opportune time to start reorganizing and get started on new project/ideas, etc. It would be inappropriate to get distracted at this time. Keep your initial intent clear and objective. Look around and realize that you have the necessary resources to achieve this important step.

2—THE HIGH PRIESTESS—FENG SHUI

DOMINANT ELEMENT: Earth

TRI GRAM: ⚏

DIRECTION: South West

The High Priestess is the second numbered card. On the Bagua, number two coincides with the earth element. The earth element is solid, reliable, and enduring. This is represented by the wall behind her consisting of stone, plaster, and clay tiles, all of which are of the earth element. We note that the ground beneath her feet is plain, unadorned earth also. The two urns on either side of her are, essentially, of the earth element in that they are made of clay. But, given their columnar structure, they also fall under the auspices of the wood element. Wood takes nourishment from earth, so the spiked palm fronds and vapor (both of the fire element) are introduced as a controlling element to temper the influence of the wood element present in The High Priestess' earth environment. It is important for The High Priestess to be centered and balanced in her site, enabling the strong foundations for her unbending faith and intuitive knowledge. In keeping with The High Priestess' sense of aloofness or detachment, the Torah from traditional Tarot cards has been replaced with a symbol more ambiguous still—a ceramic pot with vapor, which represents the veiled knowledge of The High Priestess.

2 —THE HIGH PRIESTESS—TAROT

CORE ASPECT: The mystery of the High Priestess extends her influence throughout your spread. One senses the depth of this card as the reading unfolds. Her mystery appears to engulf the surrounding cards and possibly influence the reader to greater depths of interpretation. Her presence urges the need to be mindful of shared confidences. Your intuition is truly an asset. Follow your feelings to success.

REVERSED CORE ASPECT: At this time there are no hidden activities behind the scene. Be self-reliant and exercise your own sense of independence. It's a good time to regroup and set new standards. The current cycle is ready for change. Lethargy and lack of interest has kept you from initiating new plans. Be analytical as you renew the old self.

CONTEMPLATION: Mystery grows as we proceed, the answer comes when we need.

REVERSED CONTEMPLATION: Answers close, we cannot see, just how near they may be.

DIRECTIVE: 1) The High Priestess is still holding her power and influence around you. Subtle vibrations are working beneath the surface. The whole situation has not yet solidified. 2) Patience will be rewarded. You may discover that you are becoming more attuned to your intuitive level as the situation begins to reveal itself to you.

REVERSED DIRECTIVE: 1) You feel that you are lacking the support you need. The relationship or situation is feeling one-sided. Need to review the whole situation. 2) Unwise to make a mountain of a molehill. Uncertainty on your part makes you feel insecure. Clarify what you need, there are no hidden factors.

3—THE EMPRESS—FENG SHUI

DOMINANT ELEMENT: Wood

TRI GRAM: ⚎

DIRECTION: East

The Empress is resplendent in her wood element. The wood element symbolizes creation, nourishment, continuous growth, and fertility. The spring storm in the background represents her water environment. In the generative order of elements water feeds wood, making possible the conditions of boundless creative potential for The Empress. The Empress represents abundance, which is portrayed with the ripe fruit and auspicious dragon motif. Green, featured on the Empress' garment, is the primary color of the wood element and is also present on the pear trees flanking her. The beautiful butterfly seen on the cuffs of her robe is symbolic of the perpetual metamorphosis, transformation, and rebirth of nature. There are twelve pearls on her headdress in keeping with the traditional portrayal of the twelve stars.

3—THE EMPRESS—TAROT

CORE ASPECT: The Empress surveys her garden and is enjoying all she sees. This is a good time and all is well. Growth and prosperity are blooming. A new and rejuvenating energy is now apparent. Fulfillment and happiness abound for those concerned. Celebration is in the air. Prayers are being answered and now is the time to share joy. Results are much higher than previously anticipated.

REVERSED CORE ASPECT: Plans have not materialized. One thing after another creates havoc on all levels. Depressing outlook makes it difficult to solve recent dilemma. Experiencing financial pressures adds to the burden. Struggling and unable to find a solution. Seek good advice to turn your life around.

CONTEMPLATION: Great improvement in your life. Joy will take you from your strife.

REVERSED CONTEMPLATION: Confused, unhappy, feeling down. Time to turn your life around.

DIRECTIVE: 1) It has been a long adventure in your quest to find the Empress' garden. Now the time has come to enjoy the results you anticipated. Everything is coming together and you can look forward to a satisfying conclusion. 2) Your efforts have not gone unnoticed. As you look back you can see that the challenge was not easy. You are to be congratulated for your persistence and hard work. Look forward to continuing success.

REVERSED DIRECTIVE: 1) Well, it certainly has not been good, as you well know! Unable to meet all the demands and obligations. Feeling overwhelmed has affected many things. 2) So much so that it is difficult to share your unhappiness. This being so, you must release yourself from this negative feeling and instigate a new plan of action.

THOUGHT TREND: As the Empress sits in the center of her garden she invites all to enter. It is an enviable place to be and is available as a result of diligent focus. Everyone knows what it takes to reach a personal level of satisfaction. The ultimate joy of experiencing the abundance of The Empress is to overcome the obstacles to get there!

4—THE EMPEROR—FENG SHUI

DOMINANT ELEMENT: Wood
TRI GRAM: ☴
DIRECTION: South East

The Emperor is the fourth card in the Major Arcana. In the fourth position of the Bagua, wood is the element and early summer the season. The Emperor is depicted standing firm and sure. He has confidence and can impose control of his environment. He also shares the powerful dragon motif along with The Empress, suggesting their connection or duality. The combination of elements The Emperor has been dealt is intrinsically weak. A wood site within a fire environment is a combination of elements that would tend to usurp the "chi" or energy of that particular site (the wood site is defined by the cacti and the fire environment is indicated by the mountain peaks). For The Emperor, the challenge put forth is to take proactive steps in maintaining strength and control and to decisively employ the proper controlling element, thereby creating balance through intellect and diligence.

4—THE EMPEROR—TAROT

CORE ASPECT: With discipline you can achieve your goal. Precise planning is called for. Settling for less could affect the structure that is now beginning. You enjoy the challenge of life. Past success has taught you that with diligence and patience you will triumph over adversity. Karmic circumstance has provided a new opportunity to achieve higher and more exciting levels. Anticipate and enjoy the rewards.

REVERSED CORE ASPECT: A sense of being overly burdened and insecure thinking prevents you from asserting control. The weight of responsibility can be overwhelming. Responsibilities need to be shared by all concerned. Regroup and discuss a new direction. Question the motives of someone who wants what you have.

CONTEMPLATION: Retain control and go ahead. Ignore the path that once you led.

REVERSED CONTEMPLATION: Without a plan where will you be? Just as miserable as you can be.

DIRECTIVE: 1) Everything has its own time to mature. That being so, avoid breaking your own rules. You created a plan, you set the time element, and now you are ready to make it happen. 2) In this disciplined mode listen to suggestions offered. All that remains is for you to keep within the boundaries, and attain your goal. Everything appears to be going as planned. If tempted to change the plan, then it might be advisable to understand both why and how.

REVERSED DIRECTIVE: 1) Try not to take upon yourself additional responsibilities for a while. Insecurity stems from lack of direction. 2) Might be wise and interesting to look into other possibilities before making your final decision. Placing your attention on things that are presently occurring could ease your dilemma.

THOUGHT TREND: It is good to be disciplined especially when you have created a sense of order. On the other hand once a situation becomes problematic then chaos sets in. It is at that time that an adjustment has to be made. When this is done, it is imperative to put a new goal in place immediately. Discipline begins the moment it is activated.

5—THE HIEROPHANT—FENG SHUI

DOMINANT ELEMENT: Earth
TRI GRAM: ☯
DIRECTION: Center

Number five on the Bagua is the center, which is earth. The Hierophant is pictured in a meditative pose, sitting atop a stone surrounded by the raked sand of a Zen rock garden. This earth site gradually blends into the encompassing earth environment. The low squared-off pines assume an earth-like quality through their form or shape, accentuating the uniformity of this enduring combination of elements. In Feng Shui, the combining of an earth site within an earth environment is a totally neutral, introspective place void of either good or bad environmental influences. From this stable place, The Fool on his journey has the freedom to take knowledge and advice from The Hierophant and decipher what can be used or discarded on his journey.

5—THE HIEROPHANT—TAROT

CORE ASPECT: A rigid situation stifles progress. You have the choice to conform or explore new possibilities. It's essential to allow creative juices to flow. Frustration can inhibit creative thinking. Consider and be prepared to discuss a possible remedy. Feeling restricted with present circumstance, decide if an alternative approach would be the answer.

REVERSED CORE ASPECT: There's a great possibility that someone may have interest in your ideas, programs, etc. Your sense of creativity is being recognized. Listen with care when interest is shown. Be open to new ventures but do not feel locked into a commitment. Your sense of freedom and expression should not be limited.

CONTEMPLATION: Need to flow, do not confine. Be who you are, just doing fine.

REVERSED CONTEMPLATION: Free to venture, go ahead. Stand on feet and not your head.

DIRECTIVE: 1) Belonging for the sake of belonging has its own limitations and rules. Discuss the possibility of expanding ideas that are amenable to all concerned. Feeling constricted prevents progress. 2) A narrow concept may prevent you from negotiation later. As long as you have a definite point of view then you can be more accepting to someone else's point of view.

REVERSED DIRECTIVE: 1) Unexpected presentation or phone call could promote new activity. Listen to the whole story before you commit. Sense of electricity is in the air and may well prove to be advantageous for all. 2) A second opportunity is in the offing. You will need to give extra time and concentration if you are interested. Could lead into something most beneficial. Before you finally decide, be sure that you are not taking too much upon yourself.

THOUGHT TREND: Many an opportunity is lost when we are busy with other things. It is always good to think things over and be discerning. Select what you know and decide how you feel about the situation. The influence of The Hierophant can be quite exhilarating—he exerts such a personal sense of freedom. At the same time he makes you very much aware of the responsibility involved.

6—THE LOVERS—FENG SHUI

DOMINANT ELEMENT: Metal
TRI GRAM: ☰
DIRECTION: North West

The water site, suggested by the blanketing snow, coexists in harmony with the metal environment, represented by the gently rounded hills and trees. (In the generative cycle of elements, metal can be melted to flow like water). In this peaceful balance of surroundings, the stage is set for the complex interplay of The Lovers. The man represents conscious intellect. By looking toward the woman, he is appealing to his subconscious, which in turn is intuitively aware of the divine guidance of the superconscious. The figure representing the superconscious dons a robe emblazoned with the double fish symbol, meaning, according to Buddhist tradition, freedom from ego, desire, and attachment. The superconscious offers an abacus, indicating calculated choice. This suggests the path of moral integrity. This card also celebrates the equal but different quality of man and woman, conscious and subconscious, and implores one to make choices from a broader, all encompassing, spiritual level.

6—THE LOVERS—TAROT

CORE ASPECT: Follow your inclination and select your higher choice. It's not advisable to make career/work changes during this period. Avoid breaking away from your normal working pattern. If an unusual offer appears too good to be true, then it probably is! Be firm in your resolution. Listen to your Higher Self, follow through with original plans. You have the foundation and it can happen! Try not to force issues. Reconsideration may be necessary. You do have choices available.

REVERSED CORE ASPECT: Your lack of determination causes friction. Unable to reach a decision. Situations building resentment. Continual opposition could cause disagreement, separation. Personal relationships under stress resulting in severance or divorce. Give more consideration to possible consequences.

CONTEMPLATION: The Higher choice is best by far. See exactly where you are.

REVERSED CONTEMPLATION: Feelings hurt and torn apart, could result in broken heart.

DIRECTIVE: 1) Ignore the temptation to cause unnecessary upset. Avoid making rash decisions especially when emotional levels are disturbed. 2) Reconcile differences and move into a new sphere of deeper understanding. Enjoy the new set of circumstances now available.

REVERSED DIRECTIVE: 1) Not the right time to create waves! Try to be all that you say you are. Reassurance will help the situation. Refuse to let a situation escalate. 2) Opposing energies now beginning to concern you. A firm decision can conclude this episode.

THOUGHT TREND: Try not to burn bridges behind you! The choice you make should improve your whole outlook. Decisions you make thereafter will promote the healing process. Emotional bruises will fade away and you will feel better about both you and the situation.

7—THE CHARIOT—FENG SHUI

DOMINANT ELEMENT: Metal

TRI GRAM:

DIRECTION: West

Returning triumphantly from battle, the warrior in his chariot considers the complexities of his experience. The natural arch on the horizon is symbolic of his metal environment. The beach that he rides along is indicative of his water site. This auspicious combination of elements is fertile ground for prosperity and a favorable site for the recognition of achievement. With his surroundings in harmony and under control, the warrior must now release emotional obstacles through self-disciplined focus and intent. The chariot's ultimate victory stems from transmuting his negative experiences into positive outcomes.

7—THE CHARIOT—TAROT

CORE ASPECT: Control is necessary at this time. Leave misunderstandings behind. Examine any feelings of false security. Additional efforts made can expedite the results you require. The conclusion of well earned effort. You have learned from past experience just how important it is to maintain a steady flow of continuing effort. Fortunate vibrations will soon impact and change your way of life.

REVERSED CORE ASPECT: It's difficult to extract oneself from a present situation. Something is not working the way you expected. Life appears to be uphill. You can sense the need for complete and total change. At this point it would be much better to try and correct the many faults incurred. Do what you have to do to improve the whole situation.

CONTEMPLATION: Take control and be the best. Very soon you'll pass the test.

REVERSED CONTEMPLATION: Need to change begin again. Leave behind and count to ten.

DIRECTIVE: 1) The Chariot indicates that a karmic cycle is currently accelerating toward a conclusion. Focus to complete this phase. Success is now possible. 2) So far, so good. You know what you want. If you are willing to put in the effort, you can get the results. Celebration will be due.

REVERSED DIRECTIVE: In the doldrums. Expending a lot of energy and getting nowhere. Spinning your wheels with no purpose. Dissatisfied with present circumstances.

Feeling restricted and unable to move on. Unreasonable attitude and a sense of unfairness makes it difficult to change—but change you must.

THOUGHT TREND: This could be the beginning of a successful venture. With careful thought, remove any obstacles. Not a good time to step on toes! Steer your energy away from interference and well-meaning support. You are now approaching completion and possible recognition of a job well done.

8—STRENGTH—FENG SHUI

DOMINANT ELEMENT: Earth

TRI GRAM: ☷

DIRECTION: Northwest

Strength is the eighth card in the Major Arcana. Number eight corresponds with the element earth on the Bagua. Pictured in this card is a figure practicing the art of Tai Chi. He is focusing and manipulating his Chi energy, maintaining inner strength and centeredness. The earth site suggested by the stone wall and bare ground is somewhat negatively affected by the presence of the wood element revealed as the pine tree and tree shadow. Also, the green color of the wall attests to the wood element's presence. This situation would tend to be favorable for the occupant only for a brief period, as eventually the wood element would draw nourishment from the earth site, depleting it of vital energy. Due to their jagged shape, the mountain peaks in the distance visible above the wall, represent the fire element. This serves as a controlling element in that it generates the element under threat—earth. This dynamic balance helps to sustain and perpetuate inner strength through the natural symbiotic harmony of nature's intelligence.

8—STRENGTH—TAROT

CORE ASPECT: An excellent time to reach deep within and draw upon that inner reserve. Lift yourself above the emotional level and try to separate from any turmoil that you may find disruptive. Observe what is happening around you. Try not to become involved, especially if you sense opposition or even hostility. You can take another direction and still achieve your purpose. Reorganize; meet the demands around you. Success is just around the corner.

REVERSED CORE ASPECT: The answer is not to succumb to pressure and negative attitude. You feel a sense of misunderstanding or injustice. Clear the air and do what you have to do. Try not to be defensive. Before situations deteriorate any further, clarify your position. Forcing issues will only hinder the situation. Complete and end dispute.

CONTEMPLATION: Inner strength will make the day. Success demands a fresh new way.

REVERSED CONTEMPLATION: Issues forced will slow life down. Being calm wins victor's crown.

DIRECTIVE: 1) There is more than one way to accomplish what is needed. Be flexible and willing to cooperate. The final result will be what you want. 2) A karmic decision is necessary. The question being can you overcome how you feel? If you decide the answer is yes, then reconciliation is possible.

REVERSED DIRECTIVE: 1) Pushing forward without question will alter your original concept. Come back to basics and restructure accordingly. 2) Take another look and try to understand why you feel blocked. Any further delay could hinder progress and cause unnecessary misunderstanding.

THOUGHT TREND: Looks like you will have to be the "man for all seasons!" A combination of peacemaker and counselor. If this plan were to get under way then it would help considerably if everyone concerned tried to understand the overall situation. Be firm and objective, rather than critical.

9—THE HERMIT—FENG SHUI

DOMINANT ELEMENT: Fire

TRI GRAM: ☲

DIRECTION: South

The Hermit is the Feng Shui master. He holds the Lo Pan, a divinatory tool used in assessing the Feng Shui qualities of a site. With this powerful tool and the red lantern, symbolic of the fire element, The Hermit offers his guidance on the slow climb to the top of the volcanic peak. This mountain peak serves as a simple but potent symbol of the fire environment. In concert with the red lantern, The Hermit creates a safe yet kinetic atmosphere for the undertaking of a most important personal journey. The epiphany of this journey is the realization that The Hermit is actually your higher self and that you have within you the power of God to assist you with faith, a shift in your perception, and taking responsibility for your actions. In endeavoring to make this spiritual climb, your introspection will not make you a recluse, but rather help light the way for others.

9—THE HERMIT—TAROT

CORE ASPECT: Embrace the light and hold on to your goal. Be realistic in devising how you intend to put your plans into action. Planning will activate the energy needed to format your success. The answers are available. Use discretion as you put your plans into motion. You are approaching new heights in career/business. You are stepping into a new world of great possibility. Avoid weakening your position with self-doubt and apprehension.

REVERSED CORE ASPECT: Your refusal to listen to good advice could prevent others from becoming interested. Open your mind to what is taking place around you. You could very well isolate yourself from the source and input of others. If you let your ego take over, you narrow your chances of succeeding. Overcome your pride and be open and forthright about this.

CONTEMPLATION: As you climb to reach the peak, remember others also seek.

REVERSED CONTEMPLATION: Feeling alone and can't connect, isolation shows effect.

DIRECTIVE: 1) Feeling at a standstill. Not quite sure what your next step should be. Ask for the help or advice you need and then move forward from there. 2) Ultimately it is up to you to move the situation ahead. Check and recheck to be sure that you have it all together. You can solve the situation by thinking it out clearly.

REVERSED DIRECTIVE: 1) Preoccupied with how others perceive you to be. Ego often prevents you from eceiving help. Focus on being who you really are. 2) Unable to communicate. Feeling isolated and alone. Feeling misunderstood and wishing to straighten out the situation.

THOUGHT TREND: It is now becoming possible to see what is ahead. This is a good time to make your plans and then solidify. Examine how you will put it all together and how to activate. Take your time—don't rush! To get the results you want, be sure that you have it all together. When ready, put in motion.

10—THE WHEEL OF FORTUNE—FENG SHUI

DOMINANT ELEMENT: Water

TRI GRAM: ☵

DIRECTION: North

The Wheel of Fortune is the tenth card in the Major Arcana. Number ten being the element water on the Bagua. The wheel is depicted hovering above a rushing river with a vague landscape fading into a mist. The river represents the continuous flow of life and the futility in resisting its currents. The wheel is portrayed as a jade ring in the form of a dragon with a pearl held before its jaws.

Travelers would cast such rings into rivers as placatory offerings to particular river deities before they crossed. The lanterns about the wheel represent the four cardinal points of the compass, the four suits of the Tarot, and the four seasons. Also, the shape of the lanterns are in their basic elemental form. For example, the Green Dragon lantern, or lantern representing east is columnar in structure, suggestive of the wood element. Whereas the White Tiger (or west) lantern is round like the rounded hills of a metal environment. Each lantern is adorned with a Chinese character, which is the symbol of its corresponding tri gram. Nature flows with effortless ease. In accepting and embracing the cyclical ups and downs of The Wheel of Fortune, be prepared to adapt to different circumstances as they occur. The ability to adapt and not resist the inevitable allows us to be open to opportunity instead of rehashing the past and clinging to the way things used to be.

10—WHEEL OF FORTUNE—TAROT

CORE ASPECT: As the Wheel of Life begins to move up, consider the changes it will bring. Although you feel the shifting, and perhaps insecurity, it is not the time to be hesitant. Go with the momentum and feel the energy beginning to surge upward. Clinging to the old will only slow down the new process. Be adaptable and look for new opportunities—they could be exactly what you seek.

REVERSED CORE ASPECT: The law of karma has been at work! Sometimes it is difficult to comprehend the sudden changes of life. Inevitably life has its own way of governing the choices we make. Analyze what has taken place and any impact the situation may have had on others. Allow yourself time to heal, time has a way of doing that. To allow a new beginning, let go of this situation.

CONTEMPLATION: Karma spins the Wheel around. What we learn is most profound.

REVERSED CONTEMPLATION: A turn for the worse; have faith, don't curse.

DIRECTIVE: 1) Be adaptable to the changing energies around you. It's the ideal time to be on the alert for new opportunities. 2) If you sense that your personal Wheel of Life is moving, you can usually take advantage of the momentum and be prepared for unusual and possibly unexpected series of events.

REVERSED DIRECTIVE: 1) Nothing lasts forever including how you feel at this time. The Wheel of Life continues to move and until you reground again, take time out to reevaluate the whole situation. 2) Be firm and learn from the past. Gather your energy together, regroup, and be ready for your next move.

THOUGHT TREND: We win some and we lose some! A destined force that is commonly referred to as karma seemingly governs the Wheel of Life. Each in his or her turn will experience the highs and lows of life. Knowing that new beginnings are both possible and inevitable, try to understand the lesson or joy that you are now experiencing.

11—JUSTICE—FENG SHUI

DOMINANT ELEMENT: Earth
TRI GRAM: ☷
DIRECTION: Southwest

The figure representing Justice stands surveying her earth site. The warm winds of early fall have picked up. The blowing dust appears almost like smoke as it rushes through the wispy pointed trees, setting them in motion, resembling dancing flames. These trees in the distance represent the fire environment, and the dusty plain in the foreground symbolizes the earth site. Fire produces earth in the generative order of elements enabling these favorable circumstances to encourage the dynamic and perpetuating flow of Chi to benefit the occupant of this site. With the aid of the pole, Justice balances the weight of the containers on her shoulder. The symbol and character on one container is yin and on the other is yang, illustrating the metaphor of balance. On the umbrella she carries all the colors of the spectrum, equal yet different. Justice will arrive at a decision that is honest and fair. Keeping in mind the fact that you receive what you give, Justice urges you to maintain the inner balance between your ego and your higher self, in order to direct your life with character and integrity. Thus creating fertile ground for the positive fruition of your most cherished intentions.

11—JUSTICE—TAROT

CORE ASPECT: The scales of Justice are both precise and exacting. You will receive what you have earned. All things considered, the balance is favorable to you. Your sense of fairness is appreciated. Knowing that you have done your very best will prove to be an asset, as you will begin to see the larger picture. Positive vibrations will create new vistas of opportunity.

REVERSED CORE ASPECT: Regardless of the circumstance, you are not able to change anything. Someone has taken advantage of your situation. Your hands have been tied and you are experiencing a sense of loss and perhaps guilt. Understanding the cause is a karmic lesson learned. Let it go and direct your energies elsewhere.

CONTEMPLATION: Looking good, its time to wait, Justice now may compensate.

REVERSED CONTEMPLATION: Emotions high, life seems unfair, feeling you don't have your share.

DIRECTIVE: 1) The power of Justice reveals itself through integrity and discipline. From past experience you have learned to rely upon your keen sense of intuition. You can now base your next step on what you've learned! 2) Positive vibratory flow now beginning. Important that you do not look back. Old familiar patterns do not fit into the new scheme of things. Use the positive energy to instigate a new and vibrant approach.

REVERSED DIRECTIVE: 1) You can now let go and look for new thought patterns to emerge. There has been a misunderstanding and consequently you have not felt heard. You are now free to go forward. 2) Your sense of injustice can really hold you back. What you have learned needs to form a new foundation.

THOUGHT TREND: The eleventh Major Arcana card is Justice. This card indicates that a decision or conclusion has or is about to be reached. From this point on, it becomes necessary to accept that Justice has now completed its course. Separate what has been learned and accept.

12—THE HANGED MAN—FENG SHUI

DOMINANT ELEMENT: Wood

TRI GRAM: ☳

DIRECTION: East

It is spring. The cherry tree is in full blossom, eluding to the promise of a bountiful harvest. This tree defines The Hanged Man's wood site. The gently flowing stream with its mist shrouded banks and vague irregular features are the components of the water environment. This harmonious combination of elements nourishes or bolsters The Hanged Man's self imposed predicament, which is not a predicament at all but a meditative way to remove himself from his worries and racing thoughts in order to gain objectivity and spiritual perspective. Because only in submitting or letting go can The Hanged Man attain enough peace of mind to prioritize and plan his next move. The presence of the fish indicate a sort of baptism, representing The Hanged Man's decision to change his perspective to seek spiritual and physical rest and refuge. In doing this, The Hanged Man rejuvenates his energy, which enables him to face the next step in his journey.

12—THE HANGED MAN—TAROT

CORE ASPECT: You have been waiting for action to commence. Some may feel you have been unconcerned or disinterested. When in reality you have been more than patient. Looks as though you have surprises coming along. Expect some changes at home or work. Get ready for a change of pace. You will enjoy the excitement, plus the decisions to follow. Looking for something new? Then you need to act now!

REVERSED CORE ASPECT: Do you have the feeling that you are moving fast but going nowhere? It is time to make room for something more. Slow down and take inventory. When you realize just how much you are missing you can make room to do all those things that have been on your waiting list. Take time to smell the flowers and establish a new formula of success.

CONTEMPLATION: Time is near, get ready now. Soon you'll know exactly how.

REVERSED CONTEMPLATION: Secure the goal and move along. Do not be tempted with a song.

DIRECTIVE: 1) Things are coming along. The temptation to change your goal could very well cause delay. Plenty of action yet to come. At this time there are plans yet to be completed. Use patience to accomplish all that you really want. 2) This waiting period will soon end. You will be aware of a new and innovative situation that will expedite your plans. During this waiting period be prepared to solidify your intent.

REVERSED DIRECTIVE: 1) As you begin to experience a new energy developing, it is an excellent time to take action. Avoid leaning on any unreliable source. Feeling obligated is not a good way to pursue what you have in mind. 2) List the priorities and proceed to establish a realistic plan. Make sure that you are not surrounding yourself with any false ideas. As karma starts to lose its grip you will find that many of the blockages begin to disappear.

THOUGHT TREND: You have been feeling a sense of delay. Try not to be overly impatient. Take a good look at what has been happening to see if you can do anything to solve how you feel. Your life path is now beginning to broaden and you will be confronted with more than one option. This being so, it would be wise to consider all possibilities in detail before plunging ahead.

13—TRANSITION—FENG SHUI

DOMINANT ELEMENT: Wood

TRI GRAM: ☴

DIRECTION: Southeast

The residual energy of the past exists only as a silhouette as the figure emerges from behind the rice paper door, invigorated and reborn. The soft light of a summer morning reveals an atmospheric landscape thick with the promise of growth. The presence of the trees define the dominant wood element. Attributes associated with the wood element—creativity, nourishment, and growth—can be realized when we release our fears and attachments and accept the future with renewed faith and energy. Only when we truly relinquish our fear of the unknown can we fully embrace our pure potentiality.

13—TRANSITION—TAROT

CORE ASPECT: Heave a sigh of relief! You are beginning to see a new you. It has not been easy to reach this point, but now you are seeing what you really desire. Facing a whole new vista of exciting new possibilities. As you become accustomed to new and refreshing energies, refuse to look back. The path you have walked, plus the experiences you have had are now behind you. Soon you will enter a cycle of joy and prosperity.

REVERSED CORE ASPECT: This has been a long cycle, exasperating and difficult. You are not quite out of the woods, yet you can feel a change coming on. Although you are not yet able to act upon certain issues, this episode of karma is now relinquishing its grip. Use this time to plan ahead. Very soon you will start to unleash projects you have had on hold. Obstacles will be removed. Remain active and wait for the moment to arrive.

CONTEMPLATION: Shed the old and leave the past—change is here, truth at last.

REVERSED CONTEMPLATION: Holding on to things long gone, leaves nothing to rely upon.

DIRECTIVE: 1) Complete change is entering your present circumstance. This card is a passport to take you to a New World of possibility. The trip may not be to your liking but nevertheless it will change your whole perspective in a positive way. 2) Transition cleanses, leaving you free to dream a new dream. Life has taught you much. As you rebirth and start again discard the old familiar pattern and be open to a new strength that will serve you well.

REVERSED DIRECTIVE: 1) Plan now to prevent any further deterioration. Recoup what you can and let go of barriers. The stalemate position can be alleviated if you so choose. 2) You cannot solve anything unless you are willing to initiate the process. Ignoring what has to be done will create a longer delay. It is still possible to negotiate and plan ahead.

THOUGHT TREND: The Transition card can often bring unexpected circumstances, which in turn may provide the impetus to conclude or finish a particular situation. Although there may be a tendency to be apprehensive regarding the Transition card, one does not necessarily have to feel this way! A whole new vista of possibility is often visible soon after the sudden impact of Transition.

14—TEMPERANCE—FENG SHUI

DOMINANT ELEMENT: Earth

TRI GRAM: ☯

DIRECTION: Center

The figure in The Temperance card dons a flowing green robe as a creative response in neutralizing an inherently imbalanced situation. The earth environment is portrayed by the rice paper wall consisting of a geometrical lined pattern and Yin-Yang symbol. The water site undulates at her feet. Earth pollutes water in the degenerative or destructive cycle of elements. Green is the symbolic color of the wood element, employed here as a controlling element by virtue of the fact that wood equalizes the threatening element (earth), establishing a dynamic equilibrium. The pouring back and forth of tea from the two cups held by the Temperance figure is symbolic of her commitment to tranquility, balance, and harmony. With moderation and patience she maintains a feeling of security, being careful not to jump to any conclusions and to take ample time with any major decisions.

14—TEMPERANCE—TAROT

CORE ASPECT: Rather than pushing ahead, consider how to keep your present situation evenly balanced. No acceleration is necessary. Keep on an even keel—this way you have full control and will be able to continue your present situation. You are to be commended for your progress to date. Using patience and the same diligent plan, you will advance without undo effort. Take the time needed to bring a happy conclusion.

REVERSED CORE ASPECT: The combination of stress and conflict can destroy the original concept. Your sense of judgment is impaired with the lack of organization. Self-imposed deadlines can give the impression of carelessness. Try to create a smooth working pattern that will ensure accuracy and satisfaction.

CONTEMPLATION: Keep in balance, no excess. Need it now to feel success.

REVERSED CONTEMPLATION: Slow down and see a different way. Hear what others have to say.

DIRECTIVE: 1) Try not to be excessive. Resist the urge to be compulsive. With patience you can look forward to expansion and success. Avoid upsetting the balance you have at this time. Be patient and hold on to your security. Too much too soon can negate the anticipated results. Easy does it, you will have your day! 2) Give yourself the time to consider the whole issue. If you are feeling rushed to make decisions it is important that you hold off until you feel absolutely sure that you are doing the right thing.

REVERSED DIRECTIVE: 1) Before any kind of agreement can be made, it is necessary to have an amicable flow of understanding. A need here to eliminate misunderstandings and clear the air. The input of stress does not help at all. Start again and review the structure. 2) The question here might be, "what is lacking?" Or to ask "how can I improve my situation?" As you review take a mental inventory and see if there is any particular adjustment needed.

THOUGHT TREND: Feel the tranquility pouring from within you. Consider how important it is to retain your equilibrium. At this time you are in control. To keep this level of tranquility try not to make any impulsive decisions at this time. Balance your thoughts and feelings before attempting any sudden urge or inclination. The way things are at this time are good, change is not recommended.

15—MATERIALISM—FENG SHUI

ELEMENT: Metal

TRI GRAM: ☰

DIRECTION: North West

The person featured in the Materialism card is defiantly grasping a stalk of bamboo. The bamboo grove and green wooden structure establish the wood site. The metal environment is delineated by the hills, trees, and clouds. This is a most unfavorable combination of elements as metal chops down wood in the destructive cycle of elements. A person in this situation would feel threatened by the environment. The self-absorbed figure of the Materialism card is too involved in material concerns to sense the intrinsic discord of his surroundings. He is displaying a large gold coin representing materialistic endeavors. Anger caused by the indulgence of the ego should not be taken out on others. The person experiencing these selfish conditions must not ignore their inner voice. Remember, ambition and proactive intent should not be confused with greed and avarice.

15—MATERIALISM—TAROT

CORE ASPECT: The sooner you put a halt to your present situation the better it will be. You have created an almost impossible position for yourself. Curtail your present trend and begin mending bridges. Indulgence has weakened your position. Conserve what you can and focus on the solution.

REVERSED CORE ASPECT: Leaning on others has placed you in a vulnerable position. Timidity has exposed more than you would like. Allow common sense plus integrity to take over. Indecision could jeopardize unless you get back into control. Feeling sorry for yourself is a luxury you cannot afford. Dig deep into your spiritual and mental resources to correct and retain your equilibrium.

CONTEMPLATION: Feel the pressure all around, decisions made are unwise and unsound.

REVERSED CONTEMPLATION: Stop and consider what to do. Know that now it's up to you.

DIRECTIVE: 1) Continuing as you are leads to one dead end after another. Fighting hard to hold on is becoming more difficult. Unable to find the answers indicates that the solution lies in taking a realistic view. 2) Unhappy with the way things are at this time. It took an enormous amount of energy to get to this point. Heavy mixtures of varying pressures have accumulated and now you are not sure how to take the next step. Although easier said than done, you can put a stop to the downward spiral and make things easier for all concerned. Be open and say it as it is.

REVERSED DIRECTIVE: 1) Although the situation has looked bleak, fortunately all is not lost. Before the situation deteriorates further begin to correct and put back a sense of order. 2) There is no better time than now to recognize the truth you feel within. You have been going from one extreme to another and it is time to start putting balance into your life. Perhaps you have been relying on other people's input. Begin to use your own resources.

THOUGHT TREND: Present circumstances need an overall consideration. Stress has filtered its way to your daily life. Whether by an outgoing influence or merely as a result of bad judgment, your control or lack of control governs this issue. Put your best foot forward and recognize that something has to change.

DOMINANT ELEMENT: Metal

TRI GRAM:

DIRECTION: West

Metal follows earth in the generative cycle of elements. But the metal environment embodied by the rounded hills and the earth site featured as the Great Wall is a tenuous balance at best. The metal environment draws energy from the earth site leading to decline and rapid decay. Also, the Great Wall, due to its seemingly unending, cutting nature, may harbor negative sha energy or chi. The key phrase of The Tower card, *rapid change,* is punctuated by tornadic activity of the storm cloud which has damaged the first Tower and cast it into shadow. This represents the inevitable breakdown of any situation considered permanent. From this adversity comes wonderful new opportunities, represented by the pristine, brightly lit second Tower with flag triumphantly flying.

16—THE TOWER—TAROT

CORE ASPECT: Karmic forces could be considered fortunate or catastrophic depending on the circumstances. The impact denotes the abrupt end of a karmic situation. This deep-rooted flow of karma, although often undetected, now becomes conspicuous and obvious. It's as though the karmic obligation of good, bad, or indifferent has traveled through a conduit of past experiences and in its impact creates the final severance of this karmic tie.

REVERSED CORE ASPECT: It is pointless to try and stop the inevitable breakdown that has already started. Be realistic and let it go. Trying to hang on will only prove to make matters worse. Make a clean break and allow reality to set in and release the old karmic tie. As the debris falls and the old Tower disintegrates avoid the impulse to sit and cry in the ruins. You are now released and the universe waits.

CONTEMPLATION: Vibrations stir, the scene is set, let them go—have no regret.

REVERSED CONTEMPLATION: Complete the karma let it go, discover what you need to know.

DIRECTIVE: 1) Release. Holding on to past negativity can only hinder new intentions. Get in stride with a new project or activity. At this point you still have the opportunity to do what you feel is right. 2) Emotional resistance is not a good idea. The only way to get the answers you want is to have a change in your attitude regarding a dispute and/or relationship. Your sense of disappointment will soon be replaced, and at that time concentrate on initiating your strengths toward new horizons.

REVERSED DIRECTIVE: 1) The higher self is working with you. As you feel the shift let the natural order of life fall into place. Be determined not to cling to situations no longer useful. 2) Make way for changing vibrations. The Tower exerts a strong pull to adjust. Reinforce or remove any signs of weakness. Otherwise plans intended may not stand the test. What is solid and worthwhile will withstand the force of The Tower.

THOUGHT TREND: The cycle of change can improve as well as alter the rhythm of life. Clearly the message of The Tower is that what is not meant to be, is now being removed. Old patterns are not easily discarded, but in doing so we discover new possibilities.

17—THE STAR—FENG SHUI

DOMINANT ELEMENT: Earth
TRI GRAM: ☷
DIRECTION: North East

The seventeenth card of the Major Arcana is The Star. On the bagua, The Star coincides with the earth element. The earth site features sandstone cliffs from which water cascades forth. This waterfall's beautiful mist mystically mirrors the stars in the evening sky. The waterfall can be considered the water environment. Earth conquers water. Although this elemental combination speaks of success, ultimately it may be detrimental. In order to create harmony, the metal wind chimes are introduced as a controlling element. The Star holds a vessel filled with spiritually cleansed healing water. This is an offering of spiritual rebirth, hope, health, and inspiration. In accepting The Star's gift, we merge with the superconscious, and in letting go of the ego, we can catch a glimpse of perfection. We can come away from this experience with the objectivity needed to be aware and truly thankful for the love and blessings in our life.

17—THE STAR—TAROT

CORE ASPECT: The powerful energy of The Star illuminates future accomplishments. You are in the right place at the right time. This fortunate symbol indicates that your present plans will mature and create joy for you and those near and dear. The Star is also indicative of healing on many levels. Powerful forces surround you. As you reflect The Star—you become The Star!

REVERSED CORE ASPECT: You have experienced a difficult period. Concentration has not been easy. Continuing challenges have affected several areas of life. Frustration and lack of energy also appear to have affected valued relationships. A sense of loss, and possibly sickness, has intervened. Use good judgment to rectify these situations. Rest before you contemplate new decisions.

CONTEMPLATION: Star is hope for all you need, gives the answer with great speed.

REVERSED CONTEMPLATION: Sense of loss, feeling low, need The Star for way to go.

DIRECTIVE: 1) The Star radiates inspiration, health, and the promise of fulfillment. Under this fortunate influence we see the possibility of many good things. The Star magnifies what we feel inside. It is there ready to activate when we make the effort to leap forward on the path of life. 2) The Star becomes more evident when we feel the need to pursue a purpose. Everyone can discover his or her own Star. Its cleansing rays penetrate the consciousness to give healing on all levels.

REVERSED DIRECTIVE: 1) Keep in mind that you still have a choice, limited though it may be. Take time out to review what you can do to turn things around. A need for healing—for self and others. 2) If you consider yourself to blame, communicate the mistake and do what you can to rectify. Feeling hopeless puts everything on hold. Worry affects health.

THOUGHT TREND: As The Star moves into a favorable position, gather your thoughts together and contemplate. Increasing energies inspire and motivate. The Star provides the light, plus the incentive to achieve your purpose. Solidify—know that you are going in the right direction.

18—THE MOON—FENG SHUI

DOMINANT ELEMENT: Fire
TRI GRAM: ☲
DIRECTION: South

The jagged mountain peaks on the horizon represent the fire environment. The placid body of water creates the water site. This is not an auspicious combination of elements. The occupant of this site could be perceived as arrogant or interfering. The introduction of the moon gate in the foreground serves as a controlling element. Consisting of earth, stone, and mortar, The Moon gate wall and steps can be considered to be of the earth element. In the degenerative cycle of elements, earth pollutes water. Therefore, the presence of The Moon gate tempers the threatening element water, alleviating the imbalance. The figure in The Moon card has set out on his own with a small lantern and the light of the full Moon to guide him. He seeks to be less dependent on others. He intuitively knows it's time to face his issues of insecurity. Out on the water alone, he must quell his fears and trust a higher consciousness.

18—THE MOON—TAROT

CORE ASPECT: You discover how easy it has become to rely upon your sharpened intuitiveness. You are beginning to be more perceptive and find that you are now in the throes of a spiritual transition. The consciousness feels inundated or compelled to explore further and develop this potential. Learn to trust your own feelings. You could be right.

REVERSED CORE ASPECT: Not a good time to take risks. Hold back from commitment until you see that the way is clear. To speak your mind could damage a relationship or negotiations to date. Wait till the right time arrives, you will know! The more you keep your control the better the end result.

CONTEMPLATION: Trust in self and follow through, intuition guides what to do.

REVERSED CONTEMPLATION: Keep in control and wait a while, you will have the winners smile.

DIRECTIVE: 1) The influence of the Moon pulls the consciousness to a deeper perception. Learn to trust your own feelings. Much is happening behind the scenes. Avoid involvement and intrigue. 2) With changing energies around you, stay firm. Take an independent approach and be forthright, especially if you do not want to be involved further.

REVERSED DIRECTIVE: 1) Imagination can run away with you. It is not the right time to be taking any unnecessary risks. It is too early to arrive at conclusions. Emotional reaction or judgment should be put on hold. 2) Patience is the answer! Holding back your point of view will prevent misunderstandings. Keep equilibrium intact and move forward.

THOUGHT TREND: Excellent time to collect your thoughts and ideas together. The influence of The Moon always has an element of surprise. Eventually you will realize that the developing energy is inclined to be beneficial for you. Patience is the key. Your time has yet to come!

19—THE SUN—FENG SHUI

DOMINANT ELEMENT: Water
TRI GRAM: ☵
DIRECTION: North

The nondescript shape of the sand dunes in the background and the presence of water demarcate the water environment. The single palm tree establishes the wood site. This ideal melding of elements sets the positive tone that is The Sun. It is a combination that supports success in both personal and business ventures, and is receptive to happiness and celebration. Embrace opportunity, be thankful. The Sun is like a moment of clarity, a moment when you sense the power, unity, and love of the universe. Anything is possible and everything is eternal. The Sun is an affirmation of attainment—may it liberate you.

19—THE SUN—TAROT

CORE ASPECT: The Sun embraces the essence of all joy and happiness. This vibrant symbol is the epitome of success be it recent, pending, or yet to manifest. If the seed of prosperity has been well planted then you will gain accordingly. Anticipate growth of personal finances and look toward new and fruitful opportunities.

REVERSED CORE ASPECT: Before putting your signature on any document, consider the consequences. You have learned the lesson of disappointment and also you know the agony of loss. Take a realistic view on life and develop some new and meaningful resolutions. All is not lost—you can still make amends and try to solve the predicament.

CONTEMPLATION: Positive sign, success to come, all is well with abundant Sun.

REVERSED CONTEMPLATION: Start again, review once more, observe what life has in store.

DIRECTIVE: 1) The positive aspect of The Sun indicates an upward trend allowing you to experience a substantial improvement, plus additional opportunity. Whatever your present status may be at this time you will find that the Sun will accelerate plans considerably. Opportune time to communicate and share your thoughts. 2) The influence of The Sun magnifies your potential. In turn, you may discover unusual opportunities in business or personal relationships. This exhilarating and vibrant energy should be put to the best use possible.

REVERSED DIRECTIVE: 1) Self-criticism can be harsh! Whatever you have allowed yourself to think has not been working for you, rather, the opposite! Be realistic, develop a new sense of objectivity. Begin to rectify situations that have been ignored or neglected. 2) Consider if and how close relationships may have been affected. Do what you can to let those around you know that you are now making every effort to change things around.

THOUGHT TREND: The powerful healing rays of The Sun penetrate all levels. To some measure, improvement begins in a meaningful way. Look forward to reorganizing and getting everything in order. With The Sun in the spread, the answer to your situation begins to take shape and the answer is "yes!"

20—JUDGMENT—FENG SHUI

DOMINANT ELEMENT: Earth
TRI GRAM: ☷
DIRECTION: South West

The twentieth card in the Major Arcana is Judgment. The primary message of this symbol is self-judgment or self-evaluation. The figure representing judgment is standing in an earth site within an earth environment, a solid, neutral, and enduring foundation that presents minimal distractions to color his judgment or bias. In his hands he holds two flowers, evoking the duality or coexistence of opposites within himself. The lily represents the purity of spirit, and the chrysanthemum symbolizes the fruition and maturity of earthly knowledge and experience. Judgment does not imply being judgmental. Judgment is the courage to look at yourself and recognize what is lacking. Judgment is being aware of how your decisions and actions effect those around you. It is having the objectivity to stand outside of conventional thinking and elicit a creative response to the situations at hand.

20—JUDGMENT—TAROT

CORE ASPECT: The Major card of Judgment can often bring an element of surprise—the realization that this strenuous chapter of your life has now closed. It has not been an easy road to this point. It can be difficult to comprehend that the roadblocks are now removed. A sense of freedom releases you from feeling continually obligated. You can take a new look at life and begin new ventures. It is an ideal time to really see just how possible it is to step into your future.

REVERSED CORE ASPECT: A feeling of unease and unrest will continue until you decide to do something about it. Rid yourself of the "poor me" complex. Self-pity will only make the situation worse. There is a big world out there. Don't be afraid to step out and experience it. Feeling low and unable to detach from old mistakes.

CONTEMPLATION: Breaking through, barrier gone, now you see how you have won.

REVERSED CONTEMPLATION: Unsure of what may next occur, follow instinct, just and fair.

DIRECTIVE: 1) Recent decisions have not been easy. A transformation is now concluding, which will release you from past obligations. You can now navigate a new course in life, which will include an element of surprise. New start beginning, expect financial improvements. 2) Create a new outlook. Great opportunity to leap forward. Unwanted ties can only serve to hinder the process. Present episode now finishing. Explore new vistas and enjoy.

REVERSED DIRECTIVE: 1) Weariness stifling your potential. Feeling burdened dulls the desire to correct the situation. See what you can do to correct the problem. Know that it is possible to shift the weight off your shoulders. Take time out and reevaluate. 2) Loneliness or sickness can exhaust natural vigor. Although you may not feel "up to it," nothing can change unless you do!

THOUGHT TREND: The old adage that "it's the darkness before the dawn" gives some insight to the Judgment card. It represents the ending and/or the beginning of various life chapters. Of course, each personal experience varies in its intensity. Some of life's chapters are full of intrigue, while others could be considered quite ordinary and perhaps mundane.

21—THE WORLD—FENG SHUI

DOMINANT ELEMENT: Wood

TRI GRAM:

DIRECTION: East

The figure representing The World stands in the center of the card. In hues of yellow and gold, suggesting her grounded earth position, she embodies the oracle of the Major Arcana. Beginning with wood, the dominant element of The World, all the elements are represented in vignettes of their basic landscape form. The rippling purple ribbon is a visual example of the chi flowing effortlessly and endlessly through all the elements or Tarot suits, emphasizing nature as cyclical and in constant flux. The World is the culmination of lessons and experience on the journey through the Major Arcana. With the release of mundane concerns and earthly security, the power, experience, and tenure to achieve a higher level of consciousness is yours to choose.

21—THE WORLD—TAROT

CORE ASPECT: In the center of your triumph and achievement you observe the world you have created. Always remindful of what it has taken to reach this peak, you now learn the secret of how to solidify the success gained. New decisions can be made, which makes you free to expand the success that is assured. Energy and effort was required to reach this level and you are now sensing that you will be called upon to assert your expertise and the responsibility is now yours. You are to be complimented for the success you have earned.

REVERSED CORE KEY: Content to have things exactly as they are! Unable to project and expand your horizons will prove to create stagnation. Your fear of change can cause important delays. Although you feel now that you rule the roost, you could lose your situation through your inability to recognize that changes are necessary. Open your mind to alternate solutions. Let others be involved and don't be afraid to let them shine also.

CONTEMPLATION: At the peak and in command, what comes next is in your hand.

REVERSED CONTEMPLATION: Holding back from trying more, time to raise potential score.

DIRECTIVE: 1) So far, so good! Continue to apply the same energy. Resting on your laurels only implies that you are now content. Maintain the momentum and the path of success will continue to expand. 2) Excellent time to consider any change in routine, home, work, or business. Keep on track, you still have important matters to consider in this cycle.

REVERSED DIRECTIVE: 1) A narrow margin between you and what you really would like to accomplish! It is almost as though you get so close, and then you are afraid to take that extra step. Go for it! 2) Tendency to remain on familiar ground. Resistance to change. You appear disinterested. Some may think you are stubborn when in fact you feel a need for caution.

THOUGHT TREND: Attaining a level of success means being totally immersed in what you have chosen to do. Risk is a lesser issue when you have the "know how," plus the impetus to complete plans or projects. Have clear sight of goals and then enter your own world of attainment and success.

THE MINOR ARCANA

WHITE TIGER – SUIT OF SWORDS

WHITE TIGER KING—FENG SHUI

ENVIRONMENT ELEMENT: Metal
SITE ELEMENT: Metal
TRI GRAM: ≡
DIRECTION: West

The King stands firm, resplendent in his regalia. His countenance commands authority. The King's dominance and control over his emotions, symbolized by the tiger, are clearly evident. In a gesture representing his letting go of defensiveness, the King has thrust the sword into the ground. The neutral and enduring conditions of a metal site contained within a metal environment create a reliable and receptive atmosphere for the King to exercise his knowledge, counsel, and control.

WHITE TIGER KING—TAROT

CORE ASPECT: A reliable and disciplined approach. Be patient, follow the rules. Avoid cutting corners if you want results.

REVERSED CORE ASPECT: Aware of restrictive energy, possibly from someone close. Difficult to defend your purpose. Limited choice. Tends to feel helpless.

CONTEMPLATION: A thinking man, cautious too, his advice helps you through.

REVERSED CONTEMPLATION: Will not bend his point of view, a rigid man and bully too.

DIRECTIVE: White Tiger King is a no nonsense man. Astute, he knows what he is doing. Keep within the parameters, follow protocol. Keep on schedule, and complete all requirements.

REVERSED DIRECTIVE: Unable to express what you are feeling. Present situation is confining. Trying to find a way to solve your predicament. Look deeper and find the flaws and rectify.

PROXIMITY: 1) MULTIPLE COURT CARDS In the spread indicate that other people are involved in this situation. 2) MULTIPLE WHITE TIGERS in a spread indicate concerns, pressure, and effort.

WHITE TIGER QUEEN—FENG SHUI

ENVIRONMENTAL ELEMENT: Metal
SITE ELEMENT: Earth
TRI GRAM: ☷
DIRECTION: West

The Queen sits with the tiger, who symbolizes emotions. The Queen has gained control of the tiger but still doesn't fully trust her. As a result of her prolonged struggle, the Queen evokes a sense of spiritual depth. The yellow ocher pottery and yellow deck upon which the Queen sits represent the earth site. The panorama of rolling hills and trees denote the metal environment. Metal follows earth in the generative cycle of elements. This scenario is well suited for the help and support offered by the Queen since the earth site tends to submit or broadcast its energy out toward the environment, as does the Queen's wisdom and counsel.

WHITE TIGER QUEEN—TAROT

CORE ASPECT: Experience has taught many lessons. Life continues to make demands. Your independence has enabled you to develop a good sense of humor.

REVERSED CORE ASPECT: Easily misunderstood. Your approach to the situation can often mislead those near. Avoid sharing confidential issues if you require total confidence.

CONTEMPLATION: On the ball, knows what to do, has independent point of view.

REVERSED CONTEMPLATION: Likes to talk and tell a tale, will tell yours too, without fail.

DIRECTIVE: Keep in step with all that is going on. Through life you have experienced many highs and lows. You are entering a refreshing change of energy. Be alert for unusual opportunity.

REVERSED DIRECTIVE: Don't let anyone pull the wool over your eyes. You are not getting the whole story. Be perceptive and heed your own counsel. Learn from the past and move on.

PROXIMITY: 1) MULTIPLE COURT CARDS in the spread indicate that other people are involved in this situation. 2) MULTIPLE WHITE TIGERS in spread indicate concerns, pressure, and effort.

WHITE TIGER KNIGHT—FENG SHUI

ENVIRONMENTAL ELEMENT: Metal
SITE ELEMENT: Wood
TRI GRAM: ☳
DIRECTION: West

The three-tiered pagoda, green tile roofs, and pine trees constitute the wood site. The surrounding landscape establishes the metal environment. The Knight, sensing the potentially malign imbalance of his surroundings, begins to accept responsibility for his situation. He initiates action and physically removes himself from the source of imbalance. The Knight is gaining some objectivity and control of his emotions. His intentions are noble, but his overbearing method is reflected in the tiger's submissive compliance.

WHITE TIGER KNIGHT—TAROT

CORE ASPECT: Powerful moving energy will propel you swiftly through the present situation. Expect support and help as you move ahead.

REVERSED CORE ASPECT: It may be necessary to put a hold on ideas until opposition is out of the way. Wait for the right time. Ensure plans are watertight before you forge ahead.

CONTEMPLATION: Powerful force to clear the way, gallant Knight can save the day!

REVERSED CONTEMPLATION: Opposition clouds your plan, timing is wrong—wait if you can.

DIRECTIVE: You can depend on this Knight. He moves swiftly to clear resisting situations. His energy helps you to confront aggravation and pending issues. He is thorough and the results are effective.

REVERSED DIRECTIVE: There is no point in rocking the boat. Don't ask for trouble. Eventually the opposition will disintegrate. Be patient, it just takes time. Resist the inclination to rush into a new situation at this time.

PROXIMITY: 1) MULTIPLE COURT CARDS in the spread indicate that other people are involved in this situation. 2) MULTIPLE WHITE TIGERS in a spread indicate concerns, pressure, and effort.

WHITE TIGER PAGE—FENG SHUI

ENVIRONMENT ELEMENT: Metal
SITE ELEMENT: Metal
TRI GRAM: ☰
DIRECTION: West

The site and environment share the same elemental form—metal. The steady balance of a metal site and metal environment set the stage for the interplay of the Page and the white tiger. In the Page's left hand is a scrolled document indicative of news or information. In the Page's right hand is a leash attached to an agitated tiger. The tiger depicted in the court cards of the White Tiger suit symbolizes emotions or emotional response. The Page, oblivious of the stable combination of site and environment, is forcibly attempting to control emotional issues. The unsuccessful wrangling of these issues leaves the Page disappointed and defensive.

WHITE TIGER PAGE—TAROT

CORE ASPECT: You do not have the whole story, thus the situation is not clear. A minor change can frustrate you. Can be to your advantage when you realize that it was not the right time anyway.

REVERSED CORE ASPECT: Immature input could deter your enthusiasm. Take another good look at the situation before going ahead. Could be due to lack of energy from self or another.

CONTEMPLATION: Not to worry this will pass, younger folks often sass.

REVERSED CONTEMPLATION: Not happy with results to date, should review, prepare to wait.

DIRECTIVE: Before you allow yourself to react prematurely, it would be better to ask what you want to know. Don't "jump the gun." Believe it or not, delay could be to your advantage. Do not settle for second best.

REVERSED DIRECTIVE: Insufficient input has created a stalemate position. Unless you are prepared to do something about it, let well alone. Someone close does not feel up to par. Let them know you are interested in how they feel.

PROXIMITY: 1) MULTIPLE COURT CARDS in the spread indicate that other people are involved in this situation. 2) MULTIPLE WHITE TIGERS in spread indicate concerns, pressure, and effort.

WHITE TIGER ACE—FENG SHUI

ENVIRONMENT ELEMENT: Metal
SITE ELEMENT: Water
TRI GRAM: ⚏
DIRECTION: West

The environmental element for the White Tiger Ace, as well as the entire White Tiger suit, is metal. In environmental form, metal manifests itself in gently curved hills, rounded trees, domed buildings, etc. Number one on the bagua correlates with the element water, this is the site element. A water site within the confines of a metal environment is an ideal combination. The tiger, alert and anxious, drinks from the stream, the flowing water representing prosperity. The tiger realizes she must plan ahead and focus energies on a new beginning. Success depends on the tiger tempering her emotions. The small bamboo shoot to the right of the tiger symbolizes the potentiality of a seed planted and nurtured, indicating to the tiger the perfect conditions for the seeds of success to come into fruition.

WHITE TIGER ACE—TAROT

CORE ASPECT: A new vibrant seed of success is now developing. Keep the focus on your new goal. This new beginning can be triumphant. Remember it is a new beginning.

REVERSED CORE ASPECT: Reevaluate the plan. Be sure to analyze before going forward. Anticipate just how you are going to make it all happen.

CONTEMPLATION: With extra push the Ace is strong, extending thrust where it belongs.

REVERSED CONTEMPLATION: Intent is good, now firm the plan, the answer now is "yes I can."

DIRECTIVE: It has been tough getting it all together. Now ideas are starting to take form. Think long term as you make your plans. Replace old anxieties with a new belief in yourself. If you want to make it happen—you can.

REVERSED DIRECTIVE: The concept you have is quite feasible. The problem could be how you tend to react when confronted with opposition. In your haste to get acceptance, you are not taking care of details.

PROXIMITY: 1) WHITE TIGER ACE WITH THE MOON: What we have here is a fortunate combination that is still sleeping! By all means continue to make plans. Allow a full two months before launching. Carry a quartz crystal to strengthen and inspire your ideas and plans. 2) WHITE TIGER ACE WITH BLACK TORTOISE FIVE: If you are willing to be competitive and thrust your ideas forward, you can be the victor! This situation could be demanding and will require your fullest attention. If you have the stamina then you can be very successful.

WHITE TIGER TWO—FENG SHUI

ENVIRONMENT ELEMENT: Metal
SITE ELEMENT: Earth
TRI GRAM: ☷
DIRECTION: West

The large stone blocking the tiger's path denotes the earth site. The earth site in conjunction with the metal environment is a sound combination, but ultimately at the expense of the site's energy. Since metal follows earth in the generative cycle of elements, the energy of the earth site would tend to flow away from the site toward the surrounding environs. This situation would be best suited for an occupant in the teaching or service trade. The Tiger is frustrated, she's not sure which way to go. She is having difficulty in taking the emotion out of her decision making process. Her mission or lesson is to block out other's opinions, listen to her own intuition, and choose the path that is right for her.

WHITE TIGER TWO—TAROT

CORE ASPECT: March to the beat of your own drum. Listen to your Higher Self. Situations have arrived that prompt you to try another way to solve the situation. Separate from emotional participation.

REVERSED CORE ASPECT: Unwise to slow down. Just be sure that your source is intact. Complete what you started and think twice before you introduce a new secondary plan.

CONTEMPLATION: Indecision holds things back, make your choice, get on track.

REVERSED CONTEMPLATION: Pace is quick, make the time, opportunity is the sign.

DIRECTIVE: This has been quite a ride. It has now become necessary to gather your thoughts and eliminate any further emotional banter. Tough though it may be, you have got the upper hand.

REVERSED DIRECTIVE: Act only when you are satisfied with the facts. You have come too far to make casual decisions. Check your resources and follow through accordingly. If the plan is firm, then a secondary choice is not optional.

PROXIMITY: 1) WHITE TIGER TWO WITH THE WORLD: As we look at this combination, we are confronted with the pungent impact of these cards. At best, there is every indication of "the best decision you ever made." The alternative suggests hesitation, taking the easy way out. 2) WHITE TIGER TWO WITH RED PHOENIX THREE: Although you have had hesitancy in knowing what to do, the choice is becoming quite obvious. Think about the choice itself, rather than the "what ifs." Further delay could negate both possibilities.

ENVIRONMENT ELEMENT: Metal
SITE ELEMENT: Wood
TRI GRAM: ☳
DIRECTION: West

Number three on the bagua corresponds to the element wood. The wood site is delineated by the tall, narrow pagoda tower and conifer trees flanking the tower on the right. In this case, the wood element is being represented by its elemental form rather than the material of which it consists. In this setting, the metal environment threatens the wood site. Metal dominates or chops down wood in the destructive cycle of elements. This discord has been remedied by the introduction of the water element in the form of a small pond. The nourishing energy of water generates the element under threat (in this case, the wood element) thereby establishing a dynamic balance. A ravine separates the tiger from this balanced scenario. This division symbolizes the emotional stress, upheaval, and loneliness caused by severance.

WHITE TIGER THREE—TAROT

CORE ASPECT: Dispute and disagreement can escalate the emotional circumstance. Sit back and listen. Try to understand. Get a grip on the whole thing and avoid upheaval.

REVERSED CORE ASPECT: Let go of your hurt before it creates an entirely difference picture. Step back or the situation becomes amplified. Do not allow yourself to make things worse.

CONTEMPLATION: Heart is heavy and pain is deep, severance causes you to weep.

REVERSED CONTEMPLATION: Not quite as bad, but bad enough! Confusion adds and makes it tough.

DIRECTIVE: The sudden change impacts all concerned. No amount of blame can alter anyone's feelings. Let the level of energy subside. Use and release.

REVERSED DIRECTIVE: You know by now that it's time to wrap it all up. It is hardly likely that anything more could be gained by anyone. To extract this interim period to contemplate anything extra is just plainly repetitious. Someone has to let it go—hopefully you can.

PROXIMITY: 1) WHITE TIGER THREE WITH THE FOOL: The point here is—there is no point! You have learned so very much, particularly about yourself. You are now in a position to consider options. Learn from your past mistakes, new choices are available but be discerning. 2) WHITE TIGER THREE WITH BLACK TORTOISE SEVEN: Your sensitivity has been on alert. For some time now you have been ruminant of a situation that you find irritating. Learning to live with it, is not the answer. Clear the air, you will be surprised how the tension dissipates.

ENVIRONMENT ELEMENT: Metal
SITE ELEMENT: Wood
TRI GRAM: ☷
DIRECTION: West

The Tiger spies potential prey through the bamboo fence. This fence defines the wood site. The rounded landscape forms in the background create the metal environment. This is not a favorable combination of elements since wood follows metal in the destructive sequence of elements. The tiger, sensing the latently dangerous imbalance of her immediate surroundings, chooses not to strike or attack her prey at this time. Due to the presence of the fence making her attack an unlikely success, the tiger contemplates her situation and decides to hold back, take her time, and strike at a more opportune time.

WHITE TIGER FOUR—TAROT

CORE ASPECT: Perfect time to stand back and see what is taking place. The changing energies are not yet solidified. Allow time to consider the whole scenario before committing further.

REVERSED CORE ASPECT: You now have the opportunity to feel like your old self again. It is time to consider the next step. Tread softly. You will be made aware if there are any stumbling blocks.

CONTEMPLATION: Biding time till you achieve, many plans you'd like to weave.

REVERSED CONTEMPLATION: Back on the ball and it's good. You'd change so much, if you could.

DIRECTIVE: Resist the urge to become attached or committed to a plan or program that might not be to your liking. While everything is still in the embryonic stage, it might be a good idea to hold off until you have more information.

REVERSED DIRECTIVE: If it's opposition you feel, you are probably right, so tread softly. At this time you have no problem in handling people or situations. Unless, of course, you attempt to walk where "Tigers fear to tread."

PROXIMITY: 1) WHITE TIGER FOUR WITH THE EMPRESS: What a great combination! Your patience is now being rewarded. The contrasts being like day and night. This situation has been long coming and richly deserved. 2) WHITE TIGER FOUR WITH RED PHOENIX SIX: Good news appears to come from nowhere. You can be sure it is heading straight to you. The versatile nature of this energy brings an element of surprise, especially with regard to the past. This could also lead you to new home, new job, new relationship, etc.

ENVIRONMENT ELEMENT: Metal
SITE ELEMENT: Earth
TRI GRAM:
DIRECTION: West

Number five lies at the center of the bagua and is considered to be of the earth element. The environmental element of the White Tiger suit is metal. While the site element will be solid and peaceful in conjunction with its environment, the occupant of this site will eventually experience the depletion of energy as the less dominant earth site succumbs to the powerful metal environment. The tiger on the stone wall, posturing and self-involved, doesn't realize the effect she has on those she comes in contact with. So the seemingly secure actions and intimidating stance of the tiger will eventually wither and grow weary. The tiger, upon realizing the self-centered ineffectiveness of her behavior, must appeal to her higher self to help her accept her errors and be more giving in her current or future relationships.

WHITE TIGER FIVE—TAROT

CORE ASPECT: Diverse energies appear to distract. Those close to you may feel neglected. Be open and considerate to those around. By all means, direct, but do not dictate.

REVERSED CORE ASPECT: Involvement can lead to emotional chaos. Reestablish and renew priorities. Correct misunderstandings and avoid emotional upset.

CONTEMPLATION: Preoccupied with own pursuit, maybe you don't give a hoot.

REVERSED CONTEMPLATION: Out of touch with those around, involved in self, not too profound.

DIRECTIVE: Use a velvet glove, not a boxing glove. Rigid control does not provide any elasticity. A lack of caring can dwindle your support system.

REVERSED DIRECTIVE: Watch that your own ego does not lead you down a blind alley. Take more interest in what is happening around you. Before any misunderstanding gets out of control, it is advisable to step in and get to the bottom of it.

PROXIMITY: 1) WHITE TIGER FIVE WITH THE LOVERS: Here you have a big turning on the road. What you do next can change your future perspective. It simply means following your higher instinct. Do the right thing, make no short cuts, and you will have it all back together again. 2) WHITE TIGER FIVE WITH BLACK TORTOISE SEVEN: Although you have plenty of distraction and the pressure continues, you cope extremely well. Your strength and fortitude is a plus. You have places to go and things to do, which will eventually prove your success.

WHITE TIGER SIX —FENG SHUI

ENVIRONMENT ELEMENT: Metal
SITE ELEMENT: Metal
TRI GRAM: ☰
DIRECTION: West

A stream divides a wood site from a metal site both within a metal environment. The wood site is defined by the tall pines, which appear unhealthy and lacking in vitality. The tiger leaps across the stream, extricating herself from the inauspicious wood site / metal environment combination to the more stable and desirable metal site suggested by the lobed plants and rounded rocks. The combination of a metal site within a metal environment is neutral and receptive. The tiger set her sights on the future and took action in leaving an unpleasant situation behind. This allowed the difficult cycle to phase out, enabling her to embrace the fresh, new circumstances before her.

WHITE TIGER SIX—TAROT

CORE ASPECT: Hard to believe, but the worst is over. Dwelling in the past will only hinder your new goals. Disconnect from past negativity and anticipate the new you.

REVERSED CORE ASPECT: Forging ahead can only makes things worse. Refuse to give in to your negative thoughts. A positive cycle change is imminent and most beneficial.

CONTEMPLATION: Painful memories linger on, this was rough—be glad it's gone.

REVERSED CONTEMPLATION: Deadlock seems to hold you tight, nothing changed, and you are right.

DIRECTIVE: As you disconnect from this difficult phase, new situations are already evolving. Unexpected opportunity relating to career and also indication of a possible trip. The "new you" will see everything in a different light.

REVERSED DIRECTIVE: A slight setback regarding plans will eventually prove to be more of an advantage. Take this time to evaluate your intentions. Your approach has undergone several changes and you may accept an exciting proposition.

PROXIMITY: 1) WHITE TIGER SIX WITH THE MAGICIAN:
This could be it—a breaking away from the norm. You have to do what you have to do. This combination has quite a punch. You will see how opportunity stretches out and provides the platform needed. What a relief! 2) WHITE TIGER SIX WITH RED PHOENIX EIGHT:
"Enough of this!" could be how you feel. You seem to be searching for something more in life. You may find it sooner than you think. Opportunity is imminent, and more so as you relinquish outstanding obligations.

WHITE TIGER SEVEN—FENG SHUI

ENVIRONMENT ELEMENT: Metal
SITE ELEMENT: Metal
TRI GRAM: ☱
DIRECTION: West

The red roof, by virtue of its color and form, can be considered to be of the fire element. Fire melts metal in the destructive cycle of elements and is threatening the stable and harmonious combination of elements present in White Tiger Seven. Seven on the Bagua coincides with the element metal. The metal site is merely suggested by the existence of the archway supporting the roof. The rest of the site is obscured by clouds. The metal environment is represented by the rolling hills, trees, and clouds making up the background. The red roof being the cause of the imbalance punctuates the tiger's predicament. Things haven't worked out the way the tiger planned and until she finds an alternate way to go, her situation will remain out of balance. The tiger feels trapped, she must summon her strength, seek guidance, and find patience in order to move forward.

WHITE TIGER SEVEN—TAROT

CORE ASPECT: The obstacle here might be your own stubborn attitude. You have already sensed that all is not well. Another point of view could really help.

REVERSED CORE ASPECT: You can make amends. With the right attitude you will receive the help you need. Someone trustworthy can help you. They will be aware of your distress signal.

CONTEMPLATION: Tried so hard, now let it go, what is left for you to show?

REVERSED CONTEMPLATION: Salvage pride—it's not that bad. Release the ego, you'll be glad.

DIRECTIVE: You win some you lose some. You could call it the price of experience. Pick up the pieces and try not to be stubborn. It's time to shrug this energy off and end this cycle. Get over it quick. You can surprise a lot of people with your new confidence.

REVERSED DIRECTIVE: Put energy into correcting this situation rather than focusing on how to save face. Considering you could get the support you need, it's just a matter of reducing your original expectation. Wrap it up and keep going forward. You can surprise a lot of people with your new confidence.

PROXIMITY: 1) WHITE TIGER SEVEN WITH THE HIGH PRIESTESS: This combination is indicative of karma subsiding. The lesson here is to cut off and wait until the knowledge received has finished its incubation. 2) WHITE TIGER SEVEN WITH RED PHOENIX TEN: All things go. You have resurfaced and old connections are now as strong as ever, if not better. The signs ahead are as clear as road signs. There is a coming together of joy that will impact those near and dear.

WHITE TIGER EIGHT—FENG SHUI

ENVIRONMENT ELEMENT: Metal
SITE ELEMENT: Earth
TRI GRAM: ☷
DIRECTION: West

The angular geometric forms, along with the mortar and stone, are the components that create the house, steps, and porch. This comprises the earth site. The curved forms in the background constitute the metal environment. The metal environment draws energy from the earth site. Combining these elements creates a weak foundation. Since the environment is usurping energy or chi from the site, the tiger has retreated into hiding, but only temporarily. She must seek counsel, be calm, and know that the fear will subside. The tiger must also trust that the appropriate time to seek a better balanced situation will soon present itself, and that liberating moment, coupled with the help and understanding of another, will motivate her to take proactive steps in dealing with and controlling emotion.

WHITE TIGER EIGHT—TAROT

CORE ASPECT: Although you may feel anxiety regarding your present situation you will discover the answer you need. Consider the reason to end the dilemma.

REVERSED CORE ASPECT: It is possible to find release from past concerns. The lesson being, not to overburden yourself at this time. Be ready to try something new.

CONTEMPLATION: Spotlight beams, feel exposed. Want escape, and pray for close.

REVERSED CONTEMPLATION: Believe it or not pressures drop, now you achieve and will not flop.

DIRECTIVE: The secret here is to get beyond the so-called reasons and get to the actual source. By doing this you can begin a new road of recovery and really get back to square one. Let the dust settle, be patient. You have to straighten things out. Remember to go back to the source.

REVERSED DIRECTIVE: As you begin to feel the tension ease, you might want to consider this whole situation as a learning process. Having just squeezed through this experience, make sure that you don't get that close again. straighten things out. Remember to go back to the source.

PROXIMITY: 1) WHITE TIGER EIGHT WITH STRENGTH: With this combination we see light at the end of the tunnel. If you can put emotion at one side you will be able to see that the obstacles can be eliminated. To make this possible, you must be willing to invest a new effort and reorganize completely. 2) WHITE TIGER EIGHT WITH BLACK TORTOISE SIX: A powerful combination, which gives the necessary jolt to shift into this new exhilarating vibration. With continued effort you will achieve your purpose. This rapid change presents good news and also an element of surprise.

WHITE TIGER NINE—FENG SHUI

ENVIRONMENT ELEMENT: Metal
SITE ELEMENT: Fire
TRI GRAM: ☲
DIRECTION: West

A fire site amidst a metal environment can be beneficial to the occupant, but detrimental to the environment. In White Tiger Nine, the metal environment is being affected by actual fire consuming the site. In Feng Shui, other manifestations of the fire element can also dominate a metal environment such as red, peaked roofs, livestock, or spiky palm trees. Due to the flames around her, the confused tiger is experiencing difficulty in being objective about the situation at hand. Although she is wrought with pressure and anxiety, she must begin to let go of the pain, worry, and emotion in order to seek a setting that's more conducive to her well-being.

WHITE TIGER NINE—TAROT

CORE ASPECT: Stress, anxiety, or illness often makes one feel helpless and overwhelmed. The pressures of life block your future vision. If you feel overburdened, try sharing your problem and ask for help.

REVERSED CORE ASPECT: With continued faith you can look forward to good news coming. Just a little more patience and you will see the end of this situation.

CONTEMPLATION: Difficult time for you and yours, when it rains, it pours.

REVERSED CONTEMPLATION: Faith itself will pull you through, no more standstills now for you.

DIRECTIVE: One card does not a spread create. Look at the surrounding cards and try to understand just how a particular card relates to another. For example, you might check to see if a situation has already occurred. If the card in question is in the crowning position, is it pending? If located in the sixth position you might question whether or not the situation could be avoided.

REVERSED DIRECTIVE: You could say, "this has been quite a trip!" Also, you may feel that everything but the kitchen sink has been thrown at you. We could use words like "challenge," and you have had your share. Good news is—you are moving into a whole new arena of positive energy.

PROXIMITY: 1) WHITE TIGER NINE WITH THE TOWER: Just what you needed. As these two cards collaborate, we see the abrupt ending of a difficult situation. Imagine, if you will, as minute by minute the clock reaches the top of the hour, and on the stroke of midnight everything changes. It becomes exciting and new. Just give yourself time. 2) WHITE TIGER NINE WITH WHITE TIGER ACE: Karma has dealt you an "Ace" and this time you can win!

ENVIRONMENT ELEMENT: Metal
SITE ELEMENT: Water
TRI GRAM: ☵
DIRECTION: West

The metal environment is illustrated by the domed hills, rounded trees, and clouds present in the background. The water site is defined by the river and waterfall in the foreground. The interaction of these elements creates an atmosphere of peace and tranquility. Uncomfortable in the water, the tiger looks back to where she has been. She still feels the full impact of deep despair and loss. She mulls over what has been lost and what has passed. When the tiger realizes she has happened upon an ideal, cleansing, balanced place she can then quickly release her attachment to the past and be focused on the present. The tenth card in a Minor Arcana suit is always a card of transition, and this river crossing serves as a baptism of change, releasing emotional baggage and starting the next cycle fresh and cleansed.

WHITE TIGER TEN—TAROT

CORE ASPECT: Life appears to be at its lowest point at this time, yet we know there is no eleventh white tiger. The Wheel of Life is beginning to turn. In the aftermath of this difficult cycle, have faith and look ahead.

REVERSED CORE ASPECT: You have experienced a karmic lesson. You will find an opportunity to explore new and unusual opportunities. It is important to let go of the past.

CONTEMPLATION: A coup de grace ends this phase, what comes next is still a maze.

REVERSED CONTEMPLATION: The aftermath still gives concern, a karmic lesson you had to learn.

DIRECTIVE: One thing for sure, this is a tough situation. Have ready and available all the help you can muster to surmount these last obstacles. Dwelling in the past only proves that you are not moving along or away from the negative circumstance. Look now for the White Tiger Ace to carve a new seed of opportunity.

REVERSED DIRECTIVE: A cycle change provides a brand new outlook. You begin to see things in a different light. At this time you may not feel inclined to accept additional responsibility, but nevertheless it is available for you. This has been quite a rollercoaster situation and you may wish to take a break for a while.

PROXIMITY: 1) WHITE TIGER TEN WITH RED PHOENIX TWO: The qualities of love, loyalty, and friendship have been tested. What you have now will remain secure and worthwhile. Regardless of how you feel, you will find a "new" security resulting from this experience. You don't have to look too far to recognize your support system. 2) WHITE TIGER TEN WITH THE HIGH PRIESTESS: "Its not over till its over." There is still plenty to be thinking about. Follow your feelings and you will get the inspiration that has been lacking. From the residue of your emotional outlook, you will feel the urge to establish another facet of your potential.

GREEN DRAGON – SUIT OF PENTACLES

GREEN DRAGON KING—FENG SHUI

ENVIRONMENT ELEMENT: Wood
SITE ELEMENT: Metal
TRI GRAM: ☰
DIRECTION: East

The King at his peak has calculated his options for correcting his imbalanced locale. Since the metal site, suggested by the rounded archway, threatens to overpower the energy of the surrounding wood environment, the King, under advisement from the green dragon, has introduced a pool with water lilies to serve as the controlling element water. Since water feeds or enhances wood, this helps counteract the destructive effects of the threatening element, thereby rendering the situation favorable.

GREEN DRAGON KING—TAROT

CORE ASPECT: Methodical and diligent. Cognizant of the responsibilities involved. Able to see the whole picture. Will provide a successful conclusion.

REVERSED CORE ASPECT: Opinionated and may attempt to skim the surface. Ignores detail and is oblivious to sensitive remarks. Can be aroused to anger if challenged.

CONTEMPLATION: Clever man knows his stuff. Financial whiz smart and tough.

REVERSED CONTEMPLATION: Talks a lot and tells his tale, has no substance, usually fails.

DIRECTIVE: Opportunity to increase your standing. Check and recheck both plan and procedure. Be methodical and ready to answer any questions. Do your homework and you can step up in the world.

REVERSED DIRECTIVE: Not too much depth here. Full of fluff and looks for an easy listener. Lacks detail, likes to hear the sound of his own voice. All in all, can be quite boring and repetitious.

PROXIMITY: 1) MULTIPLE COURT CARDS in the spread indicate that other people are in involved in this situation. 2) MULTIPLE GREEN DRAGONS indicate monetary transactions, loans, banking, and other financial situations.

GREEN DRAGON QUEEN—FENG SHUI

ENVIRONMENT ELEMENT: Wood
SITE ELEMENT: Earth
TRI GRAM: ☷
DIRECTION: East

The tri gram assigned to the Queen is K'un, meaning mother or mature woman. This tri gram corresponds with earth on the bagua, designating her site element as such. The ever-present mountains in the distance represent the wood environment. The Queen sits, conjuring up a creative plan to either balance her situation or move on. She knows that the dominant energy of the wood environment can weaken the chi of her earth site. This would not serve to encourage the chi to gently meander, but would instead rapidly deplete or deflect it. The dragon is present at the Queen's side should she become despondent and need encouragement or motivation.

GREEN DRAGON QUEEN—TAROT

CORE ASPECT: Creative ability and not afraid of hard work. Prefers the right atmosphere to be productive. Needs to be alone to use talents under certain conditions.

REVERSED CORE ASPECT: Will look to others for support. Due to insecure feelings, can become suspicious of those around. Often questions the motives of others due to lack of confidence.

CONTEMPLATION: Likes her space and atmosphere, to do those things she holds dear.

REVERSED CONTEMPLATION: Seeks support, yet questions all, will jump all over if you fall.

DIRECTIVE: The Green Dragon Queen has an air of mystery! Protective of home and family, yet she can separate and become totally immersed into her career/business. Highly talented, able to diversify her expertise.

REVERSED DIRECTIVE: Inclined to lean on those who support her. Relies on information she gleans from others. She is not always what she purports to be. She has developed a persona that can be misleading once you know her.

PROXIMITY: 1) MULTIPLE COURT CARDS in the spread indicate that other people are involved in this situation. 2) MULTIPLE GREEN DRAGONS indicate monetary transactions, loans, banking, and other financial situations.

GREEN DRAGON KNIGHT—FENG SHUI

ENVIRONMENT ELEMENT: Wood
SITE ELEMENT: Wood
TRI GRAM:
DIRECTION: East

The bamboo grove establishes the wood site. The physical form of the mountains in the background elude to the wood environment. This particular conjoining of elements is neutral and at peace. The Knight stands determined. He has been thorough and diligent in his travels so far and now has arrived at this point. The dragon, sensing that the Knight may require some direction, makes a suggestion that helps motivate the Knight to apply his talents and keep him moving forward.

GREEN DRAGON KNIGHT—TAROT

CORE ASPECT: Always ready to defend the underdog. Solid kind of personality, but does not find it easy to try new and different things. He thrives on encouragement from others. Loyal and reliable.

REVERSED CORE ASPECT: Impatience and dissatisfaction hinders progress. Needs continual motivation. Should develop patience. Always looking for new endeavors.

CONTEMPLATION: Holds the vision of what could be. Protects ideals and lets you see.

REVERSED CONTEMPLATION: Always looking but does not find nothing concrete comes to mind.

DIRECTIVE: You could consider the Green Dragon Knight as the bulldog of this suit! You are the master; he readily responds. Loyal and steadfast, he can bring exactly what you need but you must be in command.

REVERSED DIRECTIVE: Everything appears to be at a standstill at this time. You are still learning the hard way. It's difficult to find what you want because you wanted it yesterday. Take time to plan a new approach.

PROXIMITY: 1) MULTIPLE COURT CARDS in the spread indicate that other people are involved in this situation. 2) Multiple Green Dragons indicate monetary transactions, loans, banking, and other financial situations.

GREEN DRAGON PAGE—FENG SHUI

ENVIRONMENT ELEMENT: Wood
SITE ELEMENT: Metal
TRI GRAM: ☱
DIRECTION: East

The tri gram for "tui," or youngest daughter, is the chosen symbol for the Page. On the bagua, this symbol is associated with the metal element. Therefore, the site element of the Green Dragon Page is also metal, delineated here by the domed hill and rounded stones. The environmental element for the Green Dragon Page and the entire Green Dragon suit is wood, defined here by the pillared mountain peaks looming in the background. Since wood follows metal in the destructive cycle of elements, this indicates that the site overpowers and tends to draw energy from the surrounding environment. In a helpful gesture, the Page offers the dragon incense to be used as a controlling element. Incense falls under the auspices of the fire element and since fire melts metal, the symbolic usage of the incense would lessen the dominant effects of the site element, metal, thereby alleviating the problem of imbalance.

GREEN DRAGON PAGE—TAROT

CORE ASPECT: Expect to hear or receive positive new information. Could be regarding a change for the better. A contact or a meeting that will be beneficial to all concerned.

REVERSE CORE ASPECT: Your point of view is not appreciated. Think before you speak, it may well save the day. Refrain from overreacting to some critical comment.

CONTEMPLATION: Waiting now for news to come, anticipate a job well done!

REVERSE CONTEMPLATION: Keep your cool and don't react, time will show you—that's a fact.

DIRECTIVE: Someone sees the whole picture and you can be pleasantly surprised with the reaction you receive. Confidence is boosted. Your perseverance has been acknowledged and admired.

REVERSE DIRECTIVE: Avoid putting your foot in your mouth! Although you feel unappreciated, it is not a good time to rebel. Keep focused and look beyond how you might feel at this time. As always, it will blow over.

PROXIMITY: 1) Multiple court cards in the spread indicate that other people are involved in this situation. 2) Multiple Green Dragons indicate monetary transactions, loans, banking, and other financial situations.

GREEN DRAGON ACE—FENG SHUI

ENVIRONMENT ELEMENT: Wood
SITE ELEMENT: Water
TRI GRAM: ☷
DIRECTION: East

The dragon is present at the water's edge. The water site, demarcated by the lapping waves, exists harmoniously with the wood environment. The wood environment encompasses the bamboo, the trees and foliage, and the tall columnar mountains in the distance. In this particular scenario the environment benefits from the site's energy or chi. Since, in the generative cycle of elements, water nourishes wood, this energy exchange is symbolic of successful ventures, monetary flow, and the inexhaustible well of currency fueling the circulation of prosperity.

GREEN DRAGON ACE—TAROT

CORE ASPECT: A new impetus to improve and expand. Indication that you are receiving important information that you will find pleasing.

REVERSED CORE ASPECT: Rushing into a situation that may not work out. Advise caution, it may not be prudent to continue.

CONTEMPLATION: Success now starts to activate, see the signs, can hardly wait.

REVERSED CONTEMPLATION: Specific plans do not exist, just ideas you can't resist!

DIRECTIVE: The information you have now becomes your passport to a successful new venture. Be sure to solidify every step of the way. Follow through and be prepared! You may have to shift schedules and/or travel.

REVERSED DIRECTIVE: At this point, it might be good to review before going further and see if you have all the facts. It's a long shot and things may not work out as you thought.

PROXIMITY: 1) GREEN DRAGON ACE WITH WHITE TIGER FOUR: An interesting combination now releases previous barriers. You are close to making your plan work. Don't give up, hang in there. Looks like a karmic cycle ending. Get ready, set, and go! 2) GREEN DRAGON ACE WITH BLACK TORTOISE FOUR: The second step now begins. You are reaching that point where you can feel comfortable and expand ideas/projects. You are moving into another phase of activity. Be ready to participate and enjoy

GREEN DRAGON TWO—FENG SHUI

ENVIRONMENT ELEMENT: Wood
SITE ELEMENT: Earth
TRI GRAM: ☷
DIRECTION: East

Wood takes nourishment from earth. Earth succumbs to wood. This combination of an earth site housed in a wood environment could flourish for a certain period of time. However, the energy of the earth site could quickly become exhausted and overrun by the environmental element wood, unless the introduction of a controlling element takes place. The dragon holds a torch in one hand and a knife in the other hand, representing two elemental options to be used as controlling elements. The fire element would serve to generate or enhance the earth element, which is the element under threat. The metal element could be employed to reduce the effects of the threatening element—wood. The dragon feels it is essential that harmony is maintained, so he hangs in there considering the elemental remedies, knowing he must make a decision in order to restore balance.

GREEN DRAGON TWO—TAROT

CORE ASPECT: Juggling or struggling between this and that. Your cycle indicates that you are ready to make a choice. You will get the support and possibly more.

REVERSED CORE ASPECT: To achieve your goal it has become necessary to change the order of things. Time to be firm with yourself and reorganize your whole schedule.

CONTEMPLATION: Separate issues fill your time, will be resolved, look for a sign!

REVERSED CONTEMPLATION: Overwhelmed, so much to do, need a plan to help you through.

DIRECTIVE: You are to be complimented for the efforts you have made. Hold on a little longer and look forward to a pleasant surprise! You are in the throes of change and will experience the relief needed.

REVERSED DIRECTIVE: It feels like one thing and then another! Try not to be disheartened. Consider how you can lighten the load. Numerous obligations make it difficult to establish a routine. Need some clearance to accomplish this.

PROXIMITY: 1) GREEN DRAGON TWO WITH THE MOON: The subtle influence of The Moon is impregnating your psyche, urging you to use your intuitive sense. Your inevitable choice is now more apparent. Follow your feelings, let your support system know that you are ready. 2) GREEN DRAGON TWO WITH RED PHOENIX FOUR: You have reached a point where you feel it necessary to reevaluate what is going on around you. Somehow you have moved away emotionally from your original focus. Get back to square one and stop spinning your wheels.

GREEN DRAGON THREE—FENG SHUI

ENVIRONMENT ELEMENT: Wood
SITE ELEMENT: Wood
TRI GRAM: ☳
DIRECTION: East

The Green Dragon suit element is wood. This establishes the elemental form of the environment. This is the third card in the Green Dragon suit. Number three on the bagua corresponds to this wood element also, designating the site as such. This steady combination of elements results in a solid foundation for recognition of worth, talent, or award. In a bold, straightforward gesture, the dragon proudly presents the stone monolith as a symbol of his achievement. The Feng Shui character on the stone represents the dragon's ability to manifest its power everywhere—on land, water, and sky.

GREEN DRAGON THREE—TAROT

CORE ASPECT: Efforts made will be recognized and appreciated. Expect continuing financial growth. Establish your skill and know-how. You can achieve the success you desire.

REVERSED CORE ASPECT: To go further necessitates more effort on your part. Focus on the basics before you attempt to climb the ladder.

CONTEMPLATION: Proven now what you can do, success begins to work for you.

REVERSED CONTEMPLATION: Too much too soon creates delay, slow down, there is another way.

DIRECTIVE: It is now becoming possible to develop and expand your ability. The opportunity is here! It's important to allocate sufficient time and energy and allow your skills to surface.

REVERSED DIRECTIVE: Ideas are good but need refining. You must look at the whole picture before forging ahead. Insufficient data or information can negate the whole process. More effort is required.

PROXIMITY:1) GREEN DRAGON THREE WITH THE CHARIOT: This dynamic combination calls for patience plus precision. The presence of these two cards in the spread signifies your life path is expanding. This exciting milestone provides much joy and satisfaction. 2) GREEN DRAGON THREE WITH BLACK TORTOISE NINE: Very close to reaching a decision! Situation that appears to have been pending for some time could now meet with a measure of approval. Be open to further discussion and prepare to be flexible, it could be advantageous.

GREEN DRAGON FOUR—FENG SHUI

ENVIRONMENT ELEMENT: Wood
SITE ELEMENT: Wood
TRI GRAM: ☰
DIRECTION: East

The steep, towering mountains in the background determine the wood environment. The gnarled evergreen trees located in the foreground define the wood site. The dragon stands firm and sure. This combination of elements may be stable, but not ideal. But this doesn't sway the dragon's conviction to work within his given environmental and site combination. The dragon feels he's made a sound decision and intends to follow it through. The dragon is in charge and thrives on being in command of all his pursuits and endeavors.

GREEN DRAGON FOUR—TAROT

CORE ASPECT: Working hard to achieve the original goal. An enjoyment of responsibility and willingness to go the extra mile. Continue to use your skills well and anticipate the pleasure of success.

REVERSED CORE ASPECT: Steer away from overspending. Establish a realistic budget. To realize your dreams, you need to be patient. You can overcome the obstacles.

CONTEMPLATION: Holding strong, good things in store, good luck is knocking on your door!

REVERSED CONTEMPLATION: Budget is strained by spending, choose a method of mending.

DIRECTIVE: You have worked hard to reach this level. Finances now are beginning to improve. Surprising turn of events could very well include unexpected increase in your financial picture.

REVERSED DIRECTIVE: In spite of opposition you can still work toward your goal. Up to now you have been confronted with several obstacles, one of which has been the lack of financial control. Try to conserve what you presently have.

PROXIMITY: 1) GREEN DRAGON FOUR WITH THE HANGED MAN: Your patience and diligence is now about to be rewarded. Be ready for action! Look beyond the apparent standstill and orchestrate your next step. You have chosen the right time to get the show on the road. 2) GREEN DRAGON FOUR WITH WHITE TIGER TEN: Stark contrast brings a metamorphic turn of events! As one phase leaves, it is replaced with the wherewithal that comes rapidly to nullify past regret or doubt. Karmic shadow is erased and replaced with The Sun!

GREEN DRAGON FIVE—FENG SHUI

ENVIRONMENT ELEMENT: Wood
SITE ELEMENT: Earth
TRI GRAM:
DIRECTION: East

The dragon, with his head held low, reaches a wall. This wall and barren ground form the earth site. Feeling blocked and defeated, the dragon can't see the rich wood environment beyond. The wood environment draws energy from the earth site, beckoning the dragon to complete his quest to scale the wall. Remaining in an earth site within a wood environment is productive only for a short while. It is important to let go and move on. The dragon is on the verge of something new and wonderful, but must hang in there and scale this self-imposed wall in order to behold the beauty of his next wide open vista...it's really just a shift in perception.

GREEN DRAGON FIVE—TAROT

CORE ASPECT: Now is the time for a mental, spiritual, and physical makeover. You are much closer to your goals than you realize. The Tree of Life is ready to bloom for you.

REVERSED CORE ASPECT: Arriving at a karmic crossroad, you are confronted with unexpected circumstance. Forget your ego and stand tall. Possible new start ahead.

CONTEMPLATION: An extra shove, another push, bird in hand beats two in bush.

REVERSED CONTEMPLATION: This too will pass. Pain subsides, hard to share the hurt inside.

DIRECTIVE: One thing after another has caused stress and concern. Review present standing. Consider the whole issue, and see what you can do to conclude and ease the situation. This cycle is finishing. Let go and begin again.

REVERSED DIRECTIVE: Repetition of unusual circumstance could lead you to feel that you have been experiencing a karmic replay of events. Whatever life lesson this may be needs your understanding so that you can put it behind you.

PROXIMITY: 1) GREEN DRAGON FIVE WITH THE SUN: With this combination you can feel assured that regardless of the present situation there will be much satisfaction and joy in the not too distant future. A wonderful turn of events puts you back on track. 2) GREEN DRAGON FIVE WITH RED PHOENIX SEVEN: Not a good time to start making new choices. Face up to the limitation of what you have and go from there. As you begin to narrow down your options you will lock into a positive approach and discover the answers.

GREEN DRAGON SIX—FENG SHUI

ENVIRONMENT ELEMENT: Wood
SITE ELEMENT: Metal
TRI GRAM: ☰
DIRECTION: East

A metal site within a wood environment is a powerful place to be, but at the expense of the environment. In the degenerative cycle of elements, metal destroys wood. The metal site is delineated by the arched passageway and small round-leafed plants. Tall conifers and pillar-like mountains create the wood environment. The dragon makes a spirited effort to control the imbalanced nature of his circumstances by employing a string of red lanterns for use as a controlling element. The lanterns are representative of the fire element and since fire destroys or melts metal, the lanterns tend to neutralize the negative effects of the metal site on the wood environment. In doing so, this renders the dragon's surroundings more conducive to the flow of good karma and directs the channels of chi in a manner to receive what is rightfully his.

GREEN DRAGON SIX —TAROT

CORE ASPECT: Efforts invested may bring surprising results. Unexpected results are produced from hard work and concentration. Fortunate cycle is beginning to emerge.

REVERSED CORE ASPECT: Feeling you are neglected or perhaps overlooked. Someone appears to be ignoring you and your potential. Consider how you can best improve your situation.

CONTEMPLATION: It all begins right here and now, you are triumphant so take a bow!

REVERSED CONTEMPLATION: Feel let down and don't agree, your question now, "How could this be?"

DIRECTIVE: What goes around comes around. Look forward to acknowledgment. You can expect a happy atmosphere surrounding this situation. Could be financial or come as a result of your ability. Whatever it is, it is good!

REVERSED DIRECTIVE: Insecurity colors the whole picture. Your disappointments filter through. An exchange of confidence results in a less than satisfactory conclusion. You placed your hopes high and feel let down.

PROXIMITY: 1) GREEN DRAGON SIX WITH THE EMPEROR: Your innate sense of discipline has brought you to a new level of security. Amidst the joy of achievement comes an immediate need to regroup. Action starts more or less right away. The next step follows quickly! 2) GREEN DRAGON SIX WITH RED PHOENIX NINE: Don't overlook this unique combination. The Green Dragon Six with the Red Phoenix Nine culminates and shifts the point of destiny in a wonderful new direction. Examine surrounding cards for a more in-depth interpretation.

GREEN DRAGON SEVEN—FENG SHUI

ENVIRONMENT ELEMENT: Wood
SITE ELEMENT: Metal
TRI GRAM: ☳
DIRECTION: East

The circular stepping-stones and all the curved and rounded components of the wall and moon gate comprise the metal site. Visible through the opening of the moon gate are the soaring, columnar mountains that form the distinctive wood environment backdrop for the entire Green Dragon suit of the Minor Arcana. This particular melding of elements falls in the destructive or degenerative cycle of elements, producing an intrinsic imbalance. The dragon pauses, taking time to contemplate and plan methods of balancing his surroundings. Patience in his decision-making will be rewarded with smart, precise ideas and a welcome change for the better.

GREEN DRAGON SEVEN—TAROT

CORE ASPECT: Finances are on the rise. Expect improvement that will enable you to plan ahead. Think it all out before your next major decision. A wise choice will bring you the results you desire.

REVERSED CORE ASPECT: A good time to improve your outlook. Anxiety can dull the picture. Slow down, evaluate the whole situation. A fresh beginning would be ideal.

CONTEMPLATION: Negotiate, but don't despair, when you need, it will be there!

REVERSED CONTEMPLATION: Anxious and impatient too, rash decisions hinder you.

DIRECTIVE: Finances are now on the mend. Too early to make a splash! Hold on to a solid base. If you are in the market for a loan this new cycle could accelerate the process. Put order into your life before you splurge.

REVERSED DIRECTIVE: Ideal time to really break away from the grips of concern and worry. Release old ideas—wipe the slate clean. Something is definitely not working. Desperation depletes and deteriorates. Make a new start now!

PROXIMITY: 1) GREEN DRAGON SEVEN WITH JUSTICE: When the Green Dragon Seven locks into Justice it is important to stop and evaluate the situation. The elasticity of karma provides an opportunity to sever undesirable situations. Consider what needs to be done and do it! 2) GREEN DRAGON SEVEN WITH BLACK TORTOISE EIGHT: Procrastination now ends. To take the fullest advantage of these two cards. It is advisable to be prepared and ready for action! The time element here is swift and the emphasis is on your willingness to make it happen.

GREEN DRAGON EIGHT—FENG SHUI

ENVIRONMENTAL ELEMENT: Wood
SITE ELEMENT: Earth
TRI GRAM: ☷
DIRECTION: East

In an effort to temper the deteriorating effects of an earth site within the confines of a wood environment, the dragon, with undeterred perseverance, has planned ahead and prepared for the future by planting red chrysanthemums. The red flowers are representative of the fire element and act as a controlling element by generating the element under threat, in this case earth, because, in the generative cycle of elements, fire burns, producing ashes or earth.

GREEN DRAGON EIGHT—TAROT

CORE ASPECT: Your personal strength and dedication will bring the results desired. Try not to lose sight of your intent. The flow of finances will improve.

REVERSED CORE ASPECT: Hasty decisions prove to slow everything down. Lack of planning will only cause further delays. Seldom can one find a shortcut to success.

CONTEMPLATION: Let nothing now deter the way, concentrate and it will pay!

REVERSED CONTEMPLATION: In a spiral, feeling trapped, this is not the road you mapped.

DIRECTIVE: You are onto something good! Whatever it is—the message is clear. Stay with it and persist. The monetary aspect will increase as you go. Stick with it. To think of "changing horses midstream" is not a good proposition.

REVERSED DIRECTIVE: Trying to keep face is draining your resources. Surface skills are inadequate. If you want to continue, then find the right way to do this. Otherwise you are wasting your time and that of others.

PROXIMITY: 1) GREEN DRAGON EIGHT WITH THE HIEROPHANT: Here we have a situation where it becomes black and white. There is no leeway between. The contrasting vibratory aspect is solid. You have either got it together or you have it all wrong. 2) GREEN DRAGON EIGHT WITH RED PHOENIX ACE: It feels good and emotionally satisfying as you begin this new phase. You have the support needed to succeed. There's a spring in your step that may suggest romance or deep satisfaction.

GREEN DRAGON NINE—FENG SHUI

ENVIRONMENT ELEMENT: Wood
SITE ELEMENT: Fire
TRI GRAM: ☲
DIRECTION: East

Number nine on the bagua coincides with the element fire. The fire site is depicted by the peaked, red, tiled roof and pointed palm trees set amidst the imposing mountains of the wood environment. This is a most favorable union of elements. This generative energy of a wood environment supporting a fire site seems almost idyllic—and is, yet the dragon still has a feeling of being incomplete. While the dragon may appear to have it all, he's still compelled to search for a resolution and an inner purpose.

GREEN DRAGON NINE—TAROT

CORE ASPECT: Perhaps your sense of security prevents you from exploring beyond your comfort zone? Expansion of ideas can improve the financial picture in a positive way.

REVERSED CORE ASPECT: Avoid the impulse to get overly involved. Contemplate all that has occurred. Cultivate your sensitivity and learn how to go above and beyond.

CONTEMPLATION: Okay, okay, but not okay! Something missing? Hard to say.

REVERSED CONTEMPLATION: A "sticky wicket" that's for sure! Intrigue entangled and insecure.

DIRECTIVE: Wanting something more in life? Hard to put your finger on it. The truth may be that you like how things are. Perhaps you need a zap of zest to add color and interest! Explore new possibilities; maybe that is all you need.

REVERSED DIRECTIVE: Whatever you do, avoid becoming involved and drawn into the difficulties of others. There is a sense of loss surrounding this situation. There is a lot to consider. Meditation may help you to understand.

PROXIMITY: 1) GREEN DRAGON NINE WITH MATERIALISM: The prime focus here is dissatisfaction. Need to detach, review, and repair. Inundated and overburdened. Time to delegate and pass to others. Make a fresh start and relinquish past and unnecessary obligations. 2) GREEN DRAGON NINE WITH BLACK TORTOISE TEN: A heavy and worrisome period is now leaving. You have undergone several changes. Your emotional level has been repeatedly challenged and you are now a gallant survivor! Much to look forward to very soon.

GREEN DRAGON TEN—FENG SHUI

ENVIRONMENT ELEMENT: Wood
SITE ELEMENT: Water
TRI GRAM: ☷
DIRECTION: East

The water site and wood environment combination is a harmonious coupling, but not the sturdiest or most secure since the site nourishes or supports the environment. The dragon has put down his stringed instrument. He relaxes in his water site and is beginning to feel secure and confident. As the dragon gazes off into the distance, he still senses a residual feeling of being distracted or slightly detached, because he knows as life changes and evolves he has the responsibility to meet new challenges with proactive steps.

GREEN DRAGON TEN—TAROT

CORE ASPECT: A true sense of security is beginning to happen. It will come together. You will be recognized for your participation in a new endeavor.

REVERSED CORE ASPECT: Refuse to be involved in a situation that is not your concern. Searching for answers that are already felt within.

CONTEMPLATION: What a ride and what a spin, you really have made life begin!

REVERSED CONTEMPLATION: Money problems plus upset, clear things up or you'll regret.

DIRECTIVE: Looks like you are becoming the king pin. Your participation is appreciated. In working toward a successful completion, the keyword now is organization.

REVERSED DIRECTION: Discussion can soon turn into argument. Be logical and objective or you could find yourself in a predicament. Don't leave yourself wide open for criticism. Take a handle on what you want to do.

PROXIMITY: 1) GREEN DRAGON TEN WITH THE STAR: Vast improvement all around. This beautiful combination opens a new vista of promise. As The Star melds with the Green Dragon Ten you will see how smoothly the situation transforms—expanding beyond expectation. 2) GREEN DRAGON TEN WITH THE WHITE TIGER THREE: Money, property, and other holdings are creating concern. Feelings are hurt and those involved are perturbed and possibly angry about the whole situation. If not resolved, it could sever the relationship and create a stalemate.

BLACK TORTOISE – SUIT OF WANDS

BLACK TORTOISE KING—FENG SHUI

ENVIRONMENTAL ELEMENT: Water
SITE ELEMENT: Metal
TRI GRAM: ☰
DIRECTION: North

The tri gram "chien" means father. This correlates with the metal element on the bagua designating the King's site as metal. The curved features present in the King's site are evocative of the metal element. The background visible through the entryway encompasses the water environment. Since water follows metal in the generative cycle of elements, the tendency of the King's site would be to yield its energy to the stronger water environment. The generous nature of the King, confident in his decisive leadership qualities and secure in his power, has no qualms with submitting power to his surrounding environment. Because of his capacity for giving, this combination of elements is well suited for his goals.

BLACK TORTOISE KING—TAROT

CORE ASPECT: Competent. Solid business ability. Review any upcoming meeting or agreement. Make sure that it's to your satisfaction.

REVERSED CORE ASPECT: Go along with your feelings. If it is doesn't feel good then withdraw. It's pointless to continue if you are dissatisfied.

CONTEMPLATION: Kindly man secure and strong, impulsive but is seldom wrong.

REVERSED CONTEMPLATION: Give the facts don't make him wait, impatient will not tolerate.

DIRECTIVE: Curb your enthusiasm until you have all the facts together. Focus on the situation at hand. You are capable and have the ability to present worthwhile ideas convincingly. Anticipate a boost in finances, could be unexpected!

REVERSED DIRECTIVE: Back off any situation that makes you feel uneasy. Imperative that you review and check before proceeding further with important issues relating to finance or business agreement.

PROXIMITY: 1) MULTIPLE COURT CARDS in the spread indicate that other people are involved in this situation. 2) MULTIPLE BLACK TORTOISES indicate changing vibrations, activities and movement.

BLACK TORTOISE QUEEN—FENG SHUI

ENVIRONMENTAL ELEMENT: Water
SITE ELEMENT: Earth
TRI GRAM: ☷
DIRECTION: North

The tri gram assigned to the Queen is "k'un" or mother. On the bagua this tri gram coincides with the earth element. The bare earth, stone wall, and flat-topped dwelling form the earth site. The expanse of water and the flowing, somewhat undefined form of the trees and hills create the water environment. Since earth over-powers water, the Queen is inspired to balance her surroundings by introducing the controlling element wood in the form of bamboo. Wood derives energy from earth and consequently softens the dominant effect of the earth site on the water environment. The Queen is open to lending help, assistance, and good advice and seeks to balance her site to draw people to her.

BLACK TORTOISE QUEEN—TAROT

CORE ASPECT: Warm and practical outlook will help eliminate unanswered questions. Be open to negotiation. Be the peacemaker. Your attractive personality attracts others.

REVERSED CORE ASPECT: Due to past emotional experiences you are inclined to restrict your point of view. It's difficult to let go of memories that still hurt.

CONTEMPLATION: Will listen well to what you say, good advice in every way.

REVERSED CONTEMPLATION: Narrow thoughts restrict the flow, see the Spread and you will know.

DIRECTIVE: Interesting activity. Be open to all suggestions especially from a someone who you find to be reliable. Enjoy exciting possibilities! Recognize the importance of all concerned.

REVERSED DIRECTIVE: Don't take things for granted. Examine how you feel. Broaden your outlook. Sharing thoughts is not recommended until you are really sure how you feel. Avoid emotional conflict.

PROXIMITY: 1) MULTIPLE COURT CARDS in the spread indicate that other people are involved in this situation. 2) MULTIPLE BLACK TORTOISES indicate changing vibrations and movement.

BLACK TORTOISE KNIGHT—FENG SHUI

ENVIRONMENTAL ELEMENT: Water

SITE ELEMENT: Wood

TRI GRAM: ☳

DIRECTION: North

The tri gram associated with the Knight is "chen" or eldest son. On the bagua, the corresponding element is wood, defining the site element as such. The environmental element is water. Since, in the generative cycle of elements, water supports or feeds wood, the resulting effect of the melding of these two particular elements would be one of success and happiness. In this supportive atmosphere the Knight has the sure footing to present advantageous thoughts and ideas to the Black Tortoise giving him the awareness and clarity to consider change.

BLACK TORTOISE KNIGHT—TAROT

CORE ASPECT: Action and change can create new possibilities. The start or conclusion of an interesting life phase, relating to home or business.

REVERSED CORE ASPECT: Holding on to situations long gone. Time to turn a new page in your life story. Indecision and emotional frustration block new avenues of possibility.

CONTEMPLATION: Young not old yet not a youth, causing change that shows the truth.

REVERSED CONTEMPLATION: Indecision blocks the way, cannot find the words to say.

DIRECTIVE: Essence of change stimulates present cycle. Can open new opportunities to relocate, reorganize or restart! Follow your feelings take advantage of propositions in the offing.

REVERSED DIRECTIVE: Feeling at a standstill. Unsure of present situation. Insecurity dampens your enthusiasm. To break away from this lethargic state of mind look deeper into what is causing the problem.

PROXIMITY: The Black Tortoise Knight has a powerful urging influence. Using his energy can alleviate self-imposed blocks thrusting all pursuits forward. 1) MULTIPLE COURT CARDS in the spread indicate that other people are involved in this situation. 2) MULTIPLE BLACK TORTOISES indicate changing vibrations, activities and movement.

BLACK TORTOISE PAGE—FENG SHUI

ENVIRONMENTAL ELEMENT: Water

SITE ELEMENT: Metal

TRI GRAM:

DIRECTION: North

The Page calls out to the Black Tortoise, reading favorable news from a letter. The tri gram for Page is "tui" which means youngest daughter. On the bagua, this tri gram coincides with the metal element. The metal site is established by the domed hill, rounded rocks, and lobed leaves of the vegetation. The water environment is delineated by the large body of water and irregular contours of the trees, hills, and mountains in the background. Water follows metal in the generative order of elements, drawing energy from the site and radiating it to the surrounding environment. This combination of elements is favorable for the transmittance of messages or news, making the Feng Shui of this site receptive to the relaying of information.

BLACK TORTOISE PAGE—TAROT

CORE ASPECT: The message here is to be open to an interesting communication. Could be a letter or phone call. Follow through, it could be to your advantage.

REVERSED CORE ASPECT: Not too happy regarding the attitude or the way things are being handled. Distinct feeling of being overlooked or ignored. Decide the next step.

CONTEMPLATION: Pleasant news is on the way, give a smile, it makes your day.

REVERSED CONTEMPLATION: News comes in and may upset, deal with it and then forget.

DIRECTIVE: You will be interested and happy regarding a communication. Be sure to respond and don't procrastinate. You could be very pleased with the results. Anticipate a happy conclusion.

REVERSED DIRECTIVE: You are not too pleased with a recent contact. Refuse to be the catalyst and stop giving energy to the situation. Consider how useless it is to continue these repeated patterns.

PROXIMITY: Notice that the Black Tortoise Page is like a match! He strikes and causes a flame to ignite. In doing so he puts light into an unexpected situation. 1) MULTIPLE COURT CARDS in the spread indicate that other people are involved in this situation. 2) MULTIPLE BLACK TORTOISES indicate changing vibrations, activities, and movement.

BLACK TORTOISE ACE—FENG SHUI

ENVIRONMENTAL ELEMENT: Water
SITE ELEMENT: Water
TRI GRAM: ☵
DIRECTION: North

The water environment is represented by the snow covered, irregularly contoured hills and randomly shaped groves of leafless trees. The water environment is the backdrop for the Black Tortoise Ace, as well as the entire Black Tortoise suit. The Black Tortoise Ace is the first card of the suit and number one coincides with the water element on the bagua. The black tortoise emerges from the cold pool as a symbolic ritual of the birth or seed of enterprise. The water site within a water environment is perfect for encouraging the seed of enterprise, because this combination of elements is stable, yet flexible and fluid. The energy evoked is that of growth and evolution.

BLACK TORTOISE ACE—TAROT

CORE ASPECT: Get ready for fresh new beginnings. Could be new career, new way of life, or good news from the family. Exciting new seed of possibility.

REVERSED CORE ASPECT: Impulsive decision could delay situation even more. Need to cultivate patience and focus your energy into the details.

CONTEMPLATION: Begin a project, don't delay, success will soon be on the way.

REVERSED CONTEMPLATION: Need to try and do it right, review again with goal in sight.

DIRECTIVE: Anticipate exciting new situations. Be ready for action. Good news changes the atmosphere. Something new developing.

REVERSED DIRECTIVE: Impatience is not the answer. Might be better to take a second look at the whole situation. Accept the waiting—try an alternate approach.

PROXIMITY: 1) BLACK TORTOISE ACE WITH THE SUN: A positive combination! Brings together a powerful formula of potential success. Focus on the original concept to achieve the level required. 2) BLACK TORTOISE ACE WITH GREEN DRAGON THREE: The start of something good! Recognition or promotion. A new status indicates a new level of responsibility.

BLACK TORTOISE TWO—FENG SHUI

ENVIRONMENTAL ELEMENT: Water
SITE ELEMENT: Earth
TRI GRAM: ☷
DIRECTION: North

An earth site situated amidst a water environment equates success, but at the environment's expense. Since earth conquers water in the destructive order of elements, a controlling element is necessary to create a setting conducive to partnership or achievement in enterprise. As a preventative measure, the tortoise has introduced the wood element by planting and nurturing bamboo in the unlikely setting of winter. Wood tends to neutralize or lessen the effect of the dominant earth element. Through the effort of his plans, courage, and foresight in balancing the situation, the tortoise has persevered and is receptive to positive partnership and interest.

BLACK TORTOISE TWO—TAROT

CORE ASPECT: Perseverance will be rewarded. Use tact and be well prepared. Do your homework on this one! Gather important details regarding an agreement or transaction.

REVERSED CORE ASPECT: Clarify before rushing ahead. If this is your idea, refuse to be intimidated. Lack of planning and insufficient thought could very well put you out of the picture.

CONTEMPLATION: Perseverance wins the day, actions show what words can't say.

REVERSED CONTEMPLATION: Clarify and clear the air. May be something you should share.

DIRECTIVE: Set the stage! The first step is to review your plans. Be open to discuss and negotiate. Flexibility on your part could bring promising results.

REVERSED DIRECTIVE: Insufficient effort causes a stalemate on the present situation. Relying on others puts you at a disadvantage. Be self-sufficient and reorganize.

PROXIMITY: 1) BLACK TORTOISE TWO WITH THE WHEEL OF FORTUNE: New level of cooperation and understanding can now be established. Monitor each step of the way. You will have the support you need. 2) BLACK TORTOISE TWO WITH WHITE TIGER FOUR: Give yourself time to adjust. You have experienced a rough patch of karma. Wonderful and new possibilities are now entering your life path!

BLACK TORTOISE THREE—FENG SHUI

ENVIRONMENTAL ELEMENT: Water
SITE ELEMENT: Wood
TRI GRAM:
DIRECTION: North

The wood site is distinguished by the birch trees atop a steep promontory overlooking the lake and undulating hills of the water environment. The water environment feeds and nourishes the wood site creating favorable and beneficial conditions for the occupant of this site. The tortoise climbs the incline, sensing the harmony of the location. It has become somewhat of a struggle to reach the top, but, looking to the water, the tortoise realizes that there is assistance available to him for future endeavors.

BLACK TORTOISE THREE—TAROT

CORE ASPECT: A fortunate cycle could promote the success you have been working for. Be open to additional and unexpected resources. Be ready to act and cooperate.

REVERSED CORE ASPECT: Scattered energy, lack of detail. This pie in the sky approach is detrimental to any venture you may experience. Foundations are necessary.

CONTEMPLATION: Ready now, support will come, new horizon brings the sun.

REVERSED CONTEMPLATION: Be aware and concentrate, certain things cannot wait.

DIRECTIVE: On the fringe ready to expand plans. Someone is observing and admires your effort. Soon you will take the next step and gain support.

REVERSED DIRECTIVE: Before you step on to shaky ground, ensure that you have it all together! You have a tendency to be careless and overly confident. Consider new approach.

PROXIMITY:

1) BLACK TORTOISE THREE WITH THE CHARIOT: Plans are now going in the right direction. Last minute changes may delay results. Keep to your original plan. You will have the support you need. 2) BLACK TORTOISE THREE WITH WHITE TIGER NINE: Difficulties from the past are now beginning to dissipate. It has not been easy. Now you are getting a handle on life. Future joy is birthing now!

BLACK TORTOISE FOUR—FENG SHUI

ENVIRONMENTAL ELEMENT: Water
SITE ELEMENT: Wood
TRI GRAM: ☵
DIRECTION: North

The fourth position on the bagua coincides with the wood element. The tortoise has reached a clearing amongst the trees in this wood site. The clear flowing nature of the water environment visible in the background submits its energy to the wood site in a peaceful symbiotic bond. In the generative cycle of elements, water is needed to sustain the growth of wood. As a result of hard work and with a sense of harmony and satisfaction, the tortoise basks in the winter sun, enjoying the fruits of his labor and looking forward to future opportunities.

BLACK TORTOISE FOUR—TAROT

CORE ASPECT: Hard work is now bringing its reward. A sense of peace prevails until the next phase begins. Soon you will be ready for the next exhilarating step. Looks good.

REVERSED CORE ASPECT: Don't be afraid to let go of your guard. Let those around know how you feel. Appreciate and try not to overlook what others contribute.

CONTEMPLATION: Life begins a new plateau, vibrant energy starts to flow.

REVERSED CONTEMPLATION: Think of others, slow the pace, life is more than just a race.

DIRECTIVE: A foundation is now in place. Solid base for career, business, or romance! From these roots can grow many interesting possibilities. Nurture well.

REVERSED DIRECTIVE: As you approach your goal, leave no one behind. Situation continues to improve. Retain this strength. Show your appreciation to all concerned.

PROXIMITY: 1) BLACK TORTOISE FOUR WITH STRENGTH: Victory is in sight with this combination! Be sure to cross your t's and dot the i's. Detail is important as you sprint forward into new success. 2) BLACK TORTOISE FOUR WITH GREEN DRAGON FIVE: This is not the time to give up! Feeling perturbed regarding another issue. Original intent can still be attained. Sustain your stamina, this too will pass.

BLACK TORTOISE FIVE—FENG SHUI

ENVIRONMENTAL ELEMENT: Water
SITE ELEMENT: Earth
TRI GRAM:
DIRECTION: North

The fifth position on the bagua is the center. The center represents the earth element. The earth site is defined by the earthen plain and low, flat-topped trees. The water environment is revealed by the body of water, waterfalls, and the snow covered hills. In the destructive cycle of elements, the dominant earth element over-powers the weaker water element. Although there is a certain power in being in the dominant earth site, it results in the lack of respect for the integrity of the water environment. Against the wind and rain, the tortoise struggles to remove himself from this inauspicious site. He knows that any power obtained from the imbalanced situation is fleeting, so, with renewed focus and determination, he sets his sites on a more positive outcome.

BLACK TORTOISE FIVE—TAROT

CORE ASPECT: This is the time you give it your best. Goals are in sight. Muster your concentration and be decisive. Share your vision and make it happen.

REVERSED CORE ASPECT: Looking back you can see that you have reached a good level and all is now beginning to make sense and provide harmony. A new and invigorating vibratory force is now beginning.

CONTEMPLATION: Every day comes something new, the pace is fast, so much to do.

REVERSED CONTEMPLATION: Relief of tension winding down, opportunity now comes around.

DIRECTIVE: Ease off, far too much wasted energy. Need to change your curricula. Revise, clarify, and share information. Put a new slant on your approach.

REVERSED DIRECTIVE: No longer feel the need to be defensive. A pleasant shift in energies helps to open up new fields of opportunity. Enjoy and participate.

PROXIMITY: 1) BLACK TORTOISE FIVE WITH LOVERS: The way to go has become obvious. Now you can create a whole new set of rules. Achieve your ultimate goal and apply a new self-discipline. 2) BLACK TORTOISE FIVE WITH RED PHOENIX FIVE: You have reached this point many times! This combination suggests that you can make that extra effort and go beyond, knowing you will achieve.

BLACK TORTOISE SIX—FENG SHUI

ENVIRONMENTAL ELEMENT: Water
SITE ELEMENT: Metal
TRI GRAM: ☰
DIRECTION: North

The Tortoise stops to consider the metal site, depicted here by the rounded stones, circular bronze gong, arched temple, and domed hill. A metal site within a water environment is not a solid combination of elements for the tortoise's thoughts of success. Since metal generates water in the generative cycle of elements, the site tends to broadcast energy to the surrounding areas. This is well-suited to the spiritual nature of this particular site, being the site of a temple, since in spiritual enterprise the goal is to radiate energy outward to reach people. But this does not serve the tortoise in his current endeavor, for he must follow his heart and keep moving forward. He needs faith to achieve the intended success and outcome of pursuits in his chosen field.

BLACK TORTOISE SIX—TAROT

CORE ASPECT: Your efforts are not unnoticed. Good news is imminent. Continue to pursue your purpose. Relationships improve with your input.

REVERSED CORE ASPECT: Get your finger off the panic button. This is not the time to feel sorry for yourself. A need to reevaluate and reinvent the new you. Tension is destructive.

CONTEMPLATION: All signals go, straight on track, success is sweet, don't look back.

REVERSED CONTEMPLATION: Don't waste time, think what to do, another way will bring you through.

DIRECTIVE: Having difficulty catching up! Just coping is not enough. Release tension. Give yourself enough space to come up with a feasible plan that works.

REVERSED DIRECTIVE: Feels like you have been running in circles. Expectations have been running high. Do your best, refuse to let ego get in the way.

PROXIMITY: 1) BLACK TORTOISE SIX WITH THE HIEROPHANT: Favorable combination. A positive connection that proves to be just what you are looking for. Like a shot out of the blue, you will be totally involved! 2) BLACK TORTOISE SIX WITH GREEN DRAGON SEVEN: You are close to reaching your goal! Take it easy and consider all sides of any proposition. Finances are now beginning to increase as this cycle kicks in.

BLACK TORTOISE SEVEN—FENG SHUI

ENVIRONMENTAL ELEMENT: Water
SITE ELEMENT: Metal
TRI GRAM: ☷
DIRECTION: West

The Black Tortoise is confronted with a moongate. The rounded form of the structure, the material composition of the actual gate, and the shape of the stones comprise the metal site. The scene beyond the gate encapsulates the water environment. In the generative order of elements the site relinquishes its energy to the environment, which, as in the Black Tortoise Six card, can be beneficial to the occupant but is also contingent upon the nature of business conducted in the site. In this case the Tortoise is traveling, seeking wisdom and success in business affairs. He must keep moving toward a situation that better suits his needs. But first the tortoise is challenged by the presence of the gate and must take time to consider his options. He must be resourceful, calm under pressure, and take definitive action in getting through the gate.

BLACK TORTOISE SEVEN—TAROT

CORE ASPECT: Difficult though it may be, it is important that you do what you have to do. You are feeling the pressure directed toward you. Hold on to your purpose and take the next step. The whole scenario will change.

REVERSED CORE ASPECT: Now is the time to believe in you. Indecision can delay or cancel further progress. Refuse to be intimidated you are stronger than you think.

CONTEMPLATION: You're worried they've locked the gate. Relax, it's never too late.

REVERSED CONTEMPLATION: Time to do what must be done. Battle over, but war not won!

DIRECTIVE: Hang on a little more, you are now approaching the last phase. Don't give up now after all the effort you have made! The best has yet to come.

REVERSED DIRECTIVE: You have what it takes, so take it! Stick to your plan. Try not to invite criticism. Delve deep—discover your inner resources.

PROXIMITY:

1) BLACK TORTOISE SEVEN WITH THE STAR: Star with the Black Tortoise Seven has a great karmic promise. Message is twofold; continued effort brings inspiring results. Celebration and joy. 2) BLACK TORTOISE SEVEN WITH GREEN DRAGON EIGHT: Good time to consider your vocation. What you feel can be very real. Persist, move forward. Accomplishment plus financial increase coming.

BLACK TORTOISE EIGHT—FENG SHUI

ENVIRONMENTAL ELEMENT: Water
SITE ELEMENT: Earth
TRI GRAM: ☷
DIRECTION: North

Number eight correlates with earth on the bagua, designating the site element as such. An earth site within a water environment is an unhappy alliance. There could be temporary growth in business affairs but to the detriment of the environment. But, with the addition of a wooden bridge introduced as a controlling element, the scene becomes balanced since wood conquers earth, thus lessening the negative effects of the earth site on the water environment. In this scenario the symbolism of the wooden bridge is that of a channel or conduit for the movement and acceleration of news concerning business matters. This also allows the tortoise to have an active route to take in achieving his goals of enterprise.

BLACK TORTOISE EIGHT—TAROT

CORE ASPECT: Focus on activity relating to business/work. Acknowledgment of progress and effort. Keep lines of communication open. Be prepared to travel.

REVERSED CORE ASPECT: Take time out to think things over, calm down. Emotional outbursts can only create more friction. Take time to think.

CONTEMPLATION: Keep on top, be in command, here and there you're in demand.

REVERSED CONTEMPLATION: Issues forced, problems make, profile low for goodness sake!

DIRECTIVE: This is the next step. Pace is quickening. Activity developing. Could be on the move ready to go. Keep your cool and enjoy the changing energy.

REVERSED DIRECTIVE: Let your confidence surface. You are now coping with the remaining frustrations. Keep emotions under control and begin to feel more secure

PROXIMITY: 1) BLACK TORTOISE EIGHT WITH THE EMPEROR: This powerful combination has a strong impact that catapults you to new heights especially in work/career. Opportunity is knocking. Be ready to act! 2) BLACK TORTOISE EIGHT WITH RED PHOENIX TWO: Look forward to a deeper and more meaningful situation. Emotions are inundated with anticipation. Exciting good news. Joy comes with surprise.

BLACK TORTOISE NINE—FENG SHUI

ENVIRONMENTAL ELEMENT: Water
SITE ELEMENT: Fire
TRI GRAM: ☵
DIRECTION: North

A fire site situated in a water environment is anything but auspicious. The spiky vegetation and the bulls represent the fire element. Any animal, or materials derived from animals, are considered to be of the fire element, chiefly because the color of blood is that of fire. In this case, the bulls are red and have sharp pointed horns emphasizing the form and color of the fire element. In order for the tortoise to maintain control of this unbalanced combination of elements, he has fashioned an earthen wall symbolically containing and protecting his affairs of enterprise. Earth (represented by the wall) pollutes or tends to diminish the threatening environmental element of water, thereby bringing a potentially dangerous situation under control. The decisive control implemented by the tortoise denotes his fair judgment and ability to have a broad view in handling his affairs.

BLACK TORTOISE NINE—TAROT

CORE ASPECT: Although confident with plans, it is still essential to maintain control. Paths of possibility begin to expand. Give consideration to forthcoming venture, it could fit right in with your plans.

REVERSED CORE ASPECT: There's not enough substance to make ideas work. Insufficient preparation negates the issue. Strengthen your intent and analyze the weak spots.

CONTEMPLATION: Open mind and stretch ideas, control of doubt clears the fears.

REVERSED CONTEMPLATION: Plan the plan before next move, take new steps that you can prove.

DIRECTIVE: Hold on, keep control. Scrutinize proposal or plan offered. Don't throw the towel in just yet! Moderation and negotiation can put things into order.

REVERSED DIRECTIVE: Present situation does not fit the bill! The choice is to redo, reconsider. Anything less will be inferior. Firm your position, clear the way.

PROXIMITY: 1) BLACK TORTOISE NINE WITH THE HANGED MAN: Use this time well and examine your feelings regarding the next possibility. Determine if you wish to continue or leave alone. It will take effort either way. 2) BLACK TORTOISE NINE WITH GREEN DRAGON SEVEN: Holding pattern is about to finish. Soon you will see a change in how you feel. If you have been waiting for a successful conclusion, it is on its way.

BLACK TORTOISE TEN—FENG SHUI

ENVIRONMENTAL ELEMENT: Water
SITE ELEMENT: Water
TRI GRAM: ☵
DIRECTION: North

A water site in conjunction with a water environment is stable yet flowing and malleable. The tortoise is on a snowy point of land that extends out into the water, seemingly facing the end of his path. Under pressure to continue his effort, the tortoise must not give up. He must be creative during this time of transition and plan his next route to continue into the future. The tortoise must trust that the seeds of enterprise he has planted will manifest at the appropriate time.

BLACK TORTOISE TEN—TAROT

CORE ASPECT: Lighten the load. Unnecessary pressures continue to distract. Set your priorities and clear the way. Believe it or not you are on the brink of your success.

REVERSED CORE ASPECT: Preoccupied with self-interest. Misuse or neglect of skill and ability. Time to look inward and consider what you are throwing away. Concentrate, time to make that new start.

CONTEMPLATION: Changing levels hang in tight, nearly home with goal in sight!

REVERSED CONTEMPLATION: Out of sync, your focus gone, losing what you thought you won!

DIRECTIVE: Feeling overloaded with added responsibilities. Relief comes with this changing cycle. Communicate and designate. Be ready to reorganize.

REVERSED DIRECTIVE: Need to break through a barrier that has developed. Slowly you have narrowed your potential. Start moving blockages—watch your life happen!

PROXIMITY: 1) BLACK TORTOISE TEN WITH THE HERMIT: Before rushing into another decision it would be wiser to assess the situation objectively. Consider how you can free yourself from obligations. 2) BLACK TORTOISE TEN WITH GREEN DRAGON ACE: Just when you needed it—expect good news. Grab the new opportunity now banging on your door. All you need is to follow through and solidify.

RED PHOENIX – SUIT OF CUPS

RED PHOENIX KING—FENG SHUI

ENVIRONMENTAL ELEMENT: Fire
SITE ELEMENT: Metal
TRI GRAM: ☰
DIRECTION: South

The King's site element is metal. The arched entryway and spherical lantern are suggestive of the metal elemental form. The spired peaks of the mountains visible through the entryway establish the fire environment. Metal follows fire in the destructive order of elements, rendering the site inauspicious unless efforts are made to control or balance the situation. Reliable and respected, the King counsels the Red Phoenix. With kindness and empathy he suggests ways to rectify the imbalance of her surroundings.

RED PHOENIX KING—TAROT

CORE ASPECT: Trustworthy and intuitive. Know how important it is to listen. Be ready to act accordingly. Direct the situation before you.

REVERSED CORE ASPECT: Disagreement will only add fuel. Withdraw from comment. Any further involvement may jeopardize the situation.

CONTEMPLATION: He cares and hears what you say, listening well, he shows the way.

REVERSED CONTEMPLATION: Best not to tangle with this man. Leave well alone, if you can.

DIRECTIVE: Avoid taking short cuts! You are well on the way to tasting success. Continue to explore. Use the best sources available. Confer with reliable supporters.

REVERSED DIRECTIVE: If you feel uneasy then back off now. Unwise to get involved, especially if you feel doubtful or uncomfortable. Let go, and consider yourself fortunate.

PROXIMITY: 1) MULTIPLE COURT CARDS in the spread indicate that other people are involved in this situation. 2) MULTIPLE RED PHOENIXES in spread touch upon loved ones, emotions, and concerns.

RED PHOENIX QUEEN—FENG SHUI

ENVIRONMENTAL ELEMENT: Fire
SITE ELEMENT: Earth
TRI GRAM: ⚏
DIRECTION: South

The site element of the Queen is earth, represented by the yellow tiles on which she sits. The sharp angular outline of the mountain ridge on the horizon defines the fire environment. In the generative cycle of elements, fire produces earth...in other words, the environment sustains the energy of the site. The Queen surveys her view in a somewhat meditative and aloof manner, intuitively sensing the perfection of this combination of elements. The Red Phoenix circles above, waiting for the appropriate moment to approach the Queen.

RED PHOENIX QUEEN—TAROT

CORE ASPECT: Tendency to absorb both sides of the story before making comment. Sensitive to the issue, yet quick to defend when injustice is apparent.

REVERSED CORE ASPECT: Lacks empathy. Any given situation is colored by unwanted opinion. Unwilling to bend. Someone may get hurt. Deception creates havoc.

CONTEMPLATION: Quick to see and understand, let this lady take command.

REVERSED CONTEMPLATION: Exaggerates her point of view, her advice is not for you.

DIRECTIVE: Has an inner sense of judgment, yet tends to lean toward the underdog. Anticipation is in the air. An unusual situation will create a great deal of joy and excitement.

REVERSED CONTEMPLATION: Keep feelings or opinions to yourself, otherwise you may regret it. Hold fast, the whole issue is changing. You will be glad that you were not involved.

PROXIMITY: 1) MULTIPLE COURT CARDS in the spread indicate that other people are involved in this situation. 2) MULTIPLE RED PHOENIXES in spread touch upon loved ones, emotions, and concerns.

RED PHOENIX KNIGHT—FENG SHUI

ENVIRONMENTAL ELEMENT: Fire
SITE ELEMENT: Wood
TRI GRAM: ☳
DIRECTION: South

The designated site element of a Knight is wood. The fire environment delineated by the mountain ridge tends to overwhelm the energy of the site and can be somewhat draining to its occupant. The Knight brings the Red Phoenix an intriguing proposal in the form of a letter. This type of communication can be considered to be of the water element. The intangible nature of things, like electricity and communication, fall under the auspices of the water element due to their formless, fluid nature. This symbolic gesture and introduction of the water element helps generate or fortify the weaker element—wood. Thereby boosting the energy of the site and intensifying the conduit of communication.

RED PHOENIX KNIGHT—TAROT

CORE ASPECT: Unseen karmic ties provide an unusual bond. Be open to interesting connections. Overcome an emotional challenge and explain in detail.

REVERSED CORE ASPECT: Before signing on the dotted line, make sure that you are feeling totally confident. Have a third party check things out. Are you getting the whole story?

CONTEMPLATION: Tempting, but you feel reserve, like to—but you need the nerve.

REVERSED CONTEMPLATION: Check it all and check once more, void mistakes you made before.

DIRECTIVE: If what you feel is okay, then don't be afraid to question. If you feel a sincere karmic connection, then surely it can withstand question or challenge.

REVERSED DIRECTIVE: Several situations are now coming together. Priorities are called for. Don't fall between the cracks. Being gullible causes distress later.

PROXIMITY: 1) MULTIPLE COURT CARDS in the spread indicate that other people are involved in this situation. 2) MULTIPLE RED PHOENIXES in spread touch upon loved ones, emotions, and concerns.

ENVIRONMENTAL ELEMENT: Fire
SITE ELEMENT: Metal
TRI GRAM: ☷
DIRECTION: South

In the destructive cycle of elements, fire melts metal. Consequently, destructive energy would tend to dominate a metal site within a fire environment. The Red Phoenix could obviously not expect favorable or successful energy from this combination of elements. But the young Page is the bearer of good news. In a helpful, cooperative gesture the Page brings water both for the phoenix to drink and also as a symbolic, controlling element to implement a sense of balance.

RED PHOENIX PAGE—TAROT

CORE ASPECT: Carrier of interesting news. Be ready to act. Unexpected excitement will change the agenda.

REVERSED CORE ASPECT: Life energies are beginning to stir again. Soon you will be in action. Don't be caught unaware.

CONTEMPLATION: Bringing news, contact made, new foundations now are laid.

REVERSED CONTEMPLATION: Someone sees you in a bind, tension leaves and you unwind.

DIRECTIVE: From this point, you can now begin to organize. Feel a sense of relief. Work on completion and be sure to respond to all communications. Life rhythm is now changing, keep a steady pace.

REVERSED DIRECTIVE: Motivation has been low. There is a light at the end of the tunnel! Shake off whatever has been holding you back. Hanging on to yesterdays just adds emphasis to the situation.

PROXIMITY: 1) MULTIPLE COURT CARDS in the spread indicate that other people are involved in this situation. 2) MULTIPLE RED PHOENIXES in spread touch upon loved ones, emotions, and concerns.

RED PHOENIX ACE—FENG SHUI

ENVIRONMENTAL ELEMENT: Fire
SITE ELEMENT: Water
TRI GRAM:
DIRECTION: South

Number one on the bagua falls under the auspices of water. The water site is defined by the aqua pool in the foreground. The fire environment serves as a backdrop for the entire Red Phoenix suit and is depicted here by the ridge of sharply peaked mountains. Without the neutralizing effect of the palm trees, which are of the wood element, the dominant water site would be at odds with the fire environment. From this dynamically balanced scenario the Red Phoenix rises from the water, cleansed with new insight and sensitivity. Ready to nurture the seed of a new beginning—joy, excitement, and love surround the Red Phoenix as she begins her journey.

RED PHOENIX ACE—TAROT

CORE ASPECT: The coming together of good things for you and yours. Old restrictions are now easing away. Begin to initiate new ideas and future plans.

REVERSED CORE ASPECT: Preoccupied with those around you. Unable to shake off a deep-rooted grudge. Need to release and change outlook.

CONTEMPLATION: Life now starts an upward trend, concerns you have begin to end.

REVERSED CONTEMPLATION: Others see how you react, unconcerned and lacking tact.

DIRECTIVE: A welcome change is now developing. You have the mental space to think things out. Use it well. New activity can be exciting. Try not to repeat past mistakes. You are entering a positive energy that can change life around.

REVERSED DIRECTIVE: Too much focus on how you feel. You lack support because you are not sufficiently interested in other people's perspectives. The support system is there but you do have to reach out, otherwise you may lose it.

PROXIMITY: 1) RED PHOENIX ACE WITH THE HIGH PRIESTESS: Something is in the works. Hold off with the details until you are sure that you have it together. You can look forward to a happy conclusion but "mums" the word until you are absolutely sure. 2) RED PHOENIX ACE WITH WHITE TIGER TWO: You really do know what to do. It may require more effort on your part but the ending result will be more satisfactory. Persist and finish what you started. Your new approach will be applauded.

ENVIRONMENTAL ELEMENT: Fire
SITE ELEMENT: Earth
TRI GRAM: ☷
DIRECTION: South

The assigned site element of the second card in the Red Phoenix suit is earth. The components of the earth site are the square stepping stones, yellow tiles, sandstone wall, and the geometric form of the building. The fire environment is represented by the mountain peaks in the background. According to the generative cycle of elements, fire burns creating ash or earth, rendering this a harmonious and peaceful coupling. With the cooperation and understanding of her mate, the Red Phoenix has come to rest at this ideal site. The bonsai tree symbolizes the fruition of a union grown from either the seeds of friendship or the seed of love.

RED PHOENIX TWO—TAROT

CORE ASPECT: A special tie between two souls helps to create the perfect situation. The essence of joy and happiness accelerates excitement. Surprises are on the way.

REVERSED CORE ASPECT: The longer discord continues the more difficult it will be to clear the air. Make the first move, otherwise the situation can only deteriorate.

CONTEMPLATION: Two of you create this flow, a winning path's the way to go.

REVERSED CONTEMPLATION: Make first move, make it right, you can win without a fight.

DIRECTIVE: A solid base has now formed. Compatibility provides a stronger tie. Two minds and two hearts with the same intent are now able to combine ideas and plans. Exciting energy stirs anticipation. Get ready!

REVERSED DIRECTIVE: A need to clear the air before a misunderstanding creates a bigger gap. Allowing the situation to deteriorate does not help. Put emotions to the side.

PROXIMITY: 1) RED PHOENIX TWO WITH THE MAGICIAN: Life appears to be working like clockwork. Your individuality is evident, so much so, that you do not hinder the cooperation that others are willing to give. You are now in the drivers seat. 2) RED PHOENIX TWO WITH BLACK TORTOISE TWO: You have a firm basis and all is well. This fortunate aspect provides what you have been working for. Ideal opportunity to get the show on the road. Be open to opportunity.

RED PHOENIX THREE—FENG SHUI

ENVIRONMENTAL ELEMENT: Fire
SITE ELEMENT: Wood
TRI GRAM:
DIRECTION: South

Number three on the bagua coincides with the wood element. The wood site is composed of lush treetops of a tropical forest. The majestic red peaked mountains, suggestive of fire in their very form, create the fire environment. Wood sustains fire in the generative order of elements. Since the site supports the environment, the tendency of the energy would be to fan out toward the surrounding environment. This giving flow of chi or energy suits the Red Phoenix well as she sits atop her tree, beaming with joy, abundance, and celebration, anticipating something special.

RED PHOENIX THREE—TAROT

CORE ASPECT: Celebration time is on the way. Enjoy the feeling and use it well. Good things are happening. Pleasant possibilities are in the cards.

REVERSED CORE ASPECT: It's important not to lose control. Self-pity is not the answer. Move forward and begin again. Try not to overindulge. Let the healing begin.

CONTEMPLATION: Anticipation, much joy to come, celebrate the hard work done.

REVERSED CONTEMPLATION: Put behind all you regret, begin again and then forget.

DIRECTIVE: Look at the spread to see the detail of what is coming your way. Something is in the latter stage of development that will be pleasing and most satisfactory. Relish the process and fulfillment.

REVERSED DIRECTIVE: This particular episode requires further discussion before moving on, as tempting as it may be to let it go. Try to think of the choices that you can now make and go on from there.

PROXIMITY: 1) RED PHOENIX THREE WITH THE FOOL: The junction of these two cards implies that a successful situation is now ready for you to establish a strong and positive decision. A successful conclusion will open new avenues of joy. 2) RED PHOENIX THREE WITH BLACK TORTOISE ACE: An interesting contact has been made. This dynamic combination of Tarot levels creates a fire beneath your enthusiasm. Changes you anticipate could very well lead to greater things.

RED PHOENIX FOUR—FENG SHUI

ENVIRONMENTAL ELEMENT: Fire
SITE ELEMENT: Wood
TRI GRAM: ☲
DIRECTION: South

The presence of the trees define the wood site. This site is housed in a fire environment delineated by the jagged mountain ridge. This is a weak combination, it offers the potential for the Red Phoenix to behave in a giving, altruistic manner similar to the Red Phoenix Three card. But in this particular case the Red Phoenix feels introverted and unmotivated. She sits in her tree, discontented and bored. She's not inspired to create balance by correcting her site with a controlling element. She needs time to reevaluate her circumstances and shift her perception.

RED PHOENIX FOUR—TAROT

CORE ASPECT: Life is urging you to participate. Old energies are being released. New choices are available. No time to procrastinate.

REVERSED CORE ASPECT: Your persistence will be rewarded. There's plenty of activity behind the scene. Your path of life is now changing.

CONTEMPLATION: Several ways that you can go, time to act and interest show.

REVERSED CONTEMPLATION: A watched kettle does not boil, patience heals all turmoil.

DIRECTIVE: It is not easy trying to decide what to do, especially if you don't really know. Formulate a plan. Put some ideas together and start there. Look at your choices and get the ball rolling.

REVERSED DIRECTIVE: Results are beginning to show. Keep on keeping on. Allocate the space and time you need to achieve your purpose. Pleasant news is developing.

PROXIMITY: 1) RED PHOENIX FOUR WITH THE EMPRESS: Your patience has been tested. You are so close to achieving an unusual opportunity. Be open to accept. This situation will possibly lead you to something that attracts you even more. Doors are now opening. 2) RED PHOENIX FOUR WITH WHITE TIGER THREE: Interesting possibilities now in the works. Keep abreast of what's going on. Get all the facts. Unexpected change could be advantageous.

RED PHOENIX FIVE—FENG SHUI

ENVIRONMENTAL ELEMENT: Fire
SITE ELEMENT: Earth
TRI GRAM:
DIRECTION: South

The highly emotional phoenix, seeking a well balanced auspicious site, lands on an earthen wall lined with clay pots. Both the wall and the pots are of the earth element and are actually made from earth. The mountains on the horizon establish the fire environment. Earth follows fire in the generative cycle of elements. Therefore an earth site within a fire environment could be considered ideal as the environment releases energy to the site in a reinforcing manner. In landing, the Red Phoenix has knocked over one of the pots, breaking it. She has become fixated with the accidental breakage and this focus on the negative only serves to bolster her feeling of hopelessness.

RED PHOENIX FIVE—TAROT

CORE ASPECT: A feeling of regret hinders the possible solution. A shift of attitude can put a different light on the situation. Decide which direction to take.

REVERSED CORE ASPECT: A good time to consider alternatives before you take the next step. The difficult period is ending. Pick up the pieces and create a new pattern.

CONTEMPLATION: Deeply sad, need time to heal, hard to share just what you feel.

REVERSED CONTEMPLATION: Time to leave the past behind, let it go, see what you find.

DIRECTIVE: You have certainly had your share of problems. Lingering in the shadow of the past prevents you from making a new and necessary start. Vibrant opportunities seem encouraging. Possible new home base or job.

REVERSED DIRECTIVE: You have reached a point where decisions are difficult. Take control, otherwise you permit others to take over. If you want to get through this situation, get in charge now—it is not too late.

PROXIMITY: 1) RED PHOENIX FIVE WITH JUSTICE: All in all, the impact of this combination steers life into a metamorphosis. Although you may feel your world has been turned upside down, you will spread new wings of joy. 2) RED PHOENIX FIVE WITH WHITE TIGER EIGHT: Combinations indicating you have experienced a sense of loss and/or emotional upset. Select The Star and place a "Ten Card Celtic Spread" over The Star to gain further insight and guidance.

RED PHOENIX SIX—FENG SHUI

ENVIRONMENTAL ELEMENT: Fire
SITE ELEMENT: Metal
TRI GRAM: ☰
DIRECTION: South

Number six on the bagua corresponds to the metal element. The archway, the rounded or lobed cactus, and the curve of the blue tile create the metal site. The looming, dominant, red mountains represent the fire environment. In the degenerative or destructive cycle of elements, fire destroys metal, rendering this combination unhappy or even dangerous. A method of controlling this unsettled combination of elements would be to introduce either the earth element or the water element. Earth generates the element under threat (metal). And water tempers the threatening element (fire). In this scenario the presence of the goldfish pond introduces the water element into the mix, thereby controlling or balancing the elemental dynamics of this situation. The Red Phoenix flies over the site recognizing it from her past. It stirs old warm memories and feelings from days gone by, and motivates her to consider how she has learned from the past and how that connection to the past affects her in the present.

RED PHOENIX SIX—TAROT

CORE ASPECT: Unexpected contact will shed a new light on life. Karmic stirrings will be encouraging. Expect something different from the norm.

REVERSED CORE ASPECT: Life appears to be testing you again. Overcome your disappointment. Be sensitive to what is yet to come. A far better proposition follows.

CONTEMPLATION: Long forgotten, yet you see, something good is meant to be.

REVERSED CONTEMPLATION: Minor setbacks, patience thin, take it easy and you can win.

DIRECTIVE: A warm karmic flow of good energy awakens pleasant possibilities. This positive trend could bring happy and rewarding results.

REVERSED DIRECTIVE: A current situation does not appear to be working out. Review your expectations and reevaluate how you are being affected.

PROXIMITY: 1) RED PHOENIX SIX WITH TEMPERANCE: The important thing here is to maintain a balance and realize that "easy does it." You are about to enjoy the positive results of karma. Avoid pushing too hard and weakening your position. 2) RED PHOENIX SIX WITH BLACK TORTOISE EIGHT: The pace quickens. Expect to be inundated with one thing after another; arrangements, meetings, interviews, or the buying of property. Good energies are moving fast, be clear on what you want.

RED PHOENIX SEVEN—FENG SHUI

ENVIRONMENTAL ELEMENT: Fire
SITE ELEMENT: Metal
TRI GRAM:
DIRECTION: South

Although the eucalyptus tree is naturally made of wood, due to its rounded, circular leaves and silvery-blue color it could also be representative of the metal element. In this scenario, the eucalyptus symbolizes the metal site and the sharply peaked red mountains form the fire environment. This is not a favorable combination of elements since metal follows fire in the destructive cycle of elements. The Red Phoenix senses intuitively the imbalance, but is confused by the presence of the dense foliage, complicating her ability to make a decision regarding her imbalanced site. Should she introduce a controlling element or just move on? It is important for the Red Phoenix to stand back and attempt to take some emotion out of the decision-making process and proceed with a solid choice.

RED PHOENIX SEVEN—TAROT

CORE ASPECT: Time for action. Reality is the key. Clear the air and be prepared for a pleasant turn of events. One situation improves another.

REVERSED CORE ASPECT: At last you recognize it has all been worthwhile. You are now beginning to see the reality of future success. Give yourself a pat on the back.

CONTEMPLATION: Many choices hard to choose, be realistic, you won't lose.

REVERSED CONTEMPLATION: Don't give up, pursue your dream, goals take root—your vision seen.

DIRECTIVE: Quite a number of choices are now before you. Decide by elimination. A realistic survey will help you reach the right conclusion. From there on you will experience success in your endeavor.

REVERSED DIRECTIVE: You made the right choice. Now follow through. If you go back now, you could regret it. The choice is good. Look forward to changes that will impact your decision in a positive way.

PROXIMITY: 1) RED PHOENIX SEVEN WITH MATERIALISM: A unique opportunity to correct past mistakes. Inner conflict regarding choices made in the past. Now you are in a position to make the right choice and feel good in doing so. 2) RED PHOENIX SEVEN WITH WHITE TIGER SIX: You can now discover a way to solve a dilemma with the input of someone that cares. A difficult situation is now ending and you will soon feel free to be your own person.

RED PHOENIX EIGHT—FENG SHUI

ENVIRONMENTAL ELEMENT: Fire
SITE ELEMENT: Earth
TRI GRAM: ☷
DIRECTION: South

The Red Phoenix stands on an open desert plain, warming her wings in the morning sun. Reminiscent of The Hierophant's rock garden, the flat rocks and earthen plain comprise the earth site. The jagged peaks in the distance depict the fire environment. An earth site contained in a fire environment is a landscape at peace. From these solid, tranquil surroundings, the Red Phoenix transcends her worldly matters and seeks her inner need. She knows that things cannot continue the way they have been as she strives to attain a higher level of spirituality.

RED PHOENIX EIGHT—TAROT

CORE ASPECT: Ready for the next phase in life. Yearning to explore hidden facets of self. Meditation will unlock the key.

REVERSED CORE ASPECT: Before proceeding further solidify your goals. Changing for the sake of change may not be the answer.

CONTEMPLATION: Time to search for what you need, the "old is old," advance with speed.

REVERSED CONTEMPLATION: Change is more than making plans. What you do next, is in your hands.

DIRECTIVE: You feel the need to make some changes. Something new perhaps? The urge to look for a deeper satisfaction causes you to examine your present status and broaden your outlook.

REVERSED DIRECTIVE: Not wise to make rash decisions at this time. Your vibrations are in the process of change. It would be better not to make any decision that may be considered final. Reconsider in three weeks.

PROXIMITY: 1) RED PHOENIX EIGHT WITH THE TOWER: Already you feel the oncoming change. Dissatisfaction and disappointment in quite a few areas. Subconsciously you are preparing to make a total change as you relinquish the old you. 2) RED PHOENIX WITH BLACK TORTOISE TWO: Due to continuous effort and perseverance you will have the opportunity to negotiate and/or interview. This means success and complete change if you are ready for it. It means letting go and starting again.

RED PHOENIX NINE—FENG SHUI

ENVIRONMENTAL ELEMENT: Fire
SITE ELEMENT: Fire
TRI GRAM: ☲
DIRECTION: South

Number nine on the bagua inter-
sects with the fire element, defining the site as such. A fire site in
conjunction with a fire environment is a very powerful, lucid
combination of elements. The
intensity of this energy could be
volatile and fleeting for the occupant of the site. However, if recognized and harnessed, it could
mean your wish will come true.

The Red Phoenix is in the moment. She is rising above the energy of
the fire site (indicated by fire as well as the pointed form of the palm
trees). Fully aware of the potential of her condition, she embraces
the force of her circumstances and knows anything is possible.

RED PHOENIX NINE—TAROT

CORE ASPECT: Often referred to as the wish card. Analyze the nature of the spread. The card position determines the timing factor of this fortunate card.

REVERSED CORE ASPECT: Each way you turn there seems to be a block. Back to the drawing board. Refine your plan. It could be exactly what you need.

CONTEMPLATION: Red Phoenix Nine flies to you, brings success to what you do.

REVERSED CONTEMPLATION: Funds are low, feel deprived, only you know how you tried.

DIRECTIVE: Exceptionally fortunate card, especially if located in the tenth Celtic position. As you delineate the spread, note placement position of the Red Phoenix Nine to determine how surrounding cards influence the reading.

REVERSED DIRECTIVE: There is a solution but it's too early to expect results. In the meantime, continue your plan. Check your diet, this will help you to feel better.

PROXIMITY: 1) RED PHOENIX NINE WITH JUDGEMENT: New and exciting changes give a sense of freedom and elasticity. Release unwanted ties. Allow creativity to flow. You have paid your dues. Enjoy this karmic gift—past restrictions are now releasing. 2) RED PHOENIX NINE WITH GREEN DRAGON SIX: Pat yourself on the back. Your effort has been observed. Looks as though you can expect a financial increase or maybe a bonus. Something good is on its way with the combination of these cards.

RED PHOENIX TEN—FENG SHUI

ENVIRONMENTAL ELEMENT: Fire
SITE ELEMENT: Water
TRI GRAM: ☵
DIRECTION: South

Ten on the bagua coincides with the element water. A water site may have dominion over the fire environment, but ultimately to the detriment of the environment. The Red Phoenix sits conspicuously atop a palm tree, drawing attention to the controlling element of wood. Wood nourishes or feeds fire, fire being the element under threat. With an aura of detachment, peacefulness, and contentment, the Red Phoenix awaits wonderful and exciting changes in a scenario purposefully mirroring the image of The Sun card.

RED PHOENIX TEN—TAROT

CORE ASPECT: True joy and contentment is becoming a realization. So much to look forward to. This is a high cycle. Celebrate and enjoy—life is good.

REVERSED CORE ASPECT: Feeling low. Negative interaction from others. Depressed and upset. Could indicate a loss of someone dear.

CONTEMPLATION: This is it! The crown is yours, life now opens many doors.

REVERSED CONTEMPLATION: Feeling loss and quite upset, feelings hurt and can't forget.

DIRECTIVE: Sudden changes lift your spirits high. This situation could cause you and yours to celebrate. Movement and activity along with the realization that everything is now coming together.

REVERSED DIRECTIVE: Feelings have been hurt. Thoughtlessness can lead to disagreement. Before the situation escalates and gets out of hand, someone should make the first move. Apologies are in order.

PROXIMITY: 1) RED PHOENIX TEN WITH THE MOON: With this unusual combination of energies you now stand on firm ground. This subtle expansion of consciousness provides a deeper awareness of what is happening around you. It may not show, but you will know. 2) RED PHOENIX TEN WITH GREEN DRAGON TWO: Much has taken place. Try not to procrastinate, think how to alleviate unnecessary obligations. Maintain equilibrium and once you have decided to—just do it. Financial status improves.

APPENDIX

THE CELTIC CROSS SPREAD

The ancient Celtic Cross Spread is deceptively simple in form. This spread has a unique ability to expose the known and the unknown, the seen and the unseen. This spread is a good starting point and should be thought of as a basic tool.

I never cease to be amazed at how ten cards can give so much information. This spread, as depicted on the next page, can be used to answer questions that require some background or general knowledge. In its simplistic form it enables the reader to explore:

1. THE.......... Now
2. THE.......... Influential Vibrations
3. THE.......... Reason
4. THE.......... Last Ten Days
5. THE.......... Possible Consequence
6. THE.......... Next Ten Days
7. THE.......... Apprehension I Feel
8. THE.......... Feelings of Others
9. THE.......... Positive Aspect
10. THE.......... Expected Results Within the Next 30 Days

THE CELTIC CROSS SPREAD

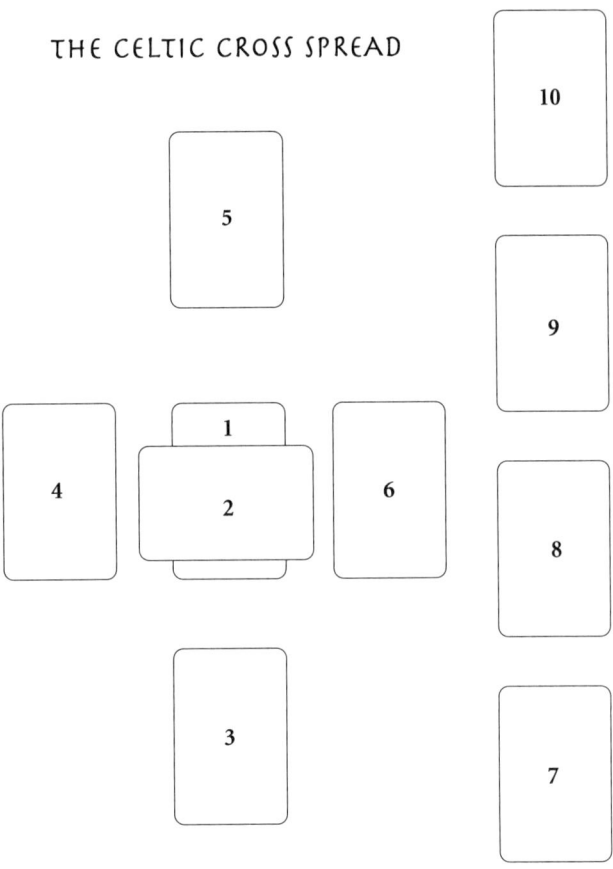

1. THE NOW

This is the "now" card, it is happening now. This first card tells you what the querent is presently experiencing. Sometimes whether he or she knows it or not!

If a court card turns up in the "now" position it would indicate that another person is involved. If it is a "Self Verification" card then you would know that "you" are the reason that this is happening now and "you" are primarily the focus.

NOTE: To avoid being repetitious throughout the spread I have left it to you the reader, to determine how, or if, you intend to recognize and use the court cards with regard to their possible multiple uses as court cards; Verification Cards, Self-Verification Cards, allocated cards etc.

2. THE INFLUENTIAL VIBRATIONS

You might want to think of this second card as the "and" card. At any one time more than one situation can be happening suggesting that the second card (crossing) is an additional situation.
If cards one and two were obviously unrelated or not seemingly connected then you would be dealing with two separate situations.

3. THE REASON

Here we have an indication of how or why the querent presented the question. Although the third card may appear totally unrelated, and your attention is more on what is happening now, it must be understood that the sequence of events that are now occurring were triggered from the situation that is represented in this third card (the basis, the root). Keep in mind that the third card has already been "activated" as a result of a previous situation.

4. THE LAST TEN DAYS

During the past ten days the client has been undergoing a mini transition. Certain issues are now beginning to dissipate. Granted, the client may not feel this way, especially if they have experienced upset or disappointment, but the energy has begun to shift and the client should be encouraged to let it go and move on.

The fourth card could also have reference to a positive situation that the client has experienced in these last ten days or so. But either way, the card in the fourth position is in reference to an energy that is now on its way out.

5. THE POSSIBLE CONSEQUENCE

As a result of efforts made or not made, the crowning energy is in the process of solidifying but has not been yet activated.

This is an ideal time to encourage the querent to use this positive energy to bring about a desired circumstance. On the other hand, if the querent is undergoing undue stress or is not thinking positively, the fifth card will reflect this and appear to prolong the situation.

The "possible consequence" becomes the result of how the querent intends to use the incoming energy. A simple interpretation would be:

If the energy is good—use it! If the querent seems to have a negative view because of a particular situation, then it is here, that the reader would try and shed more light on the problem to help the querent solve the dilemma.

6. THE NEXT TEN DAYS

When you analyze the sixth card I suggest that you also consider the tenth card. These two cards have a connection—one leads to the other. When you delineate the complete spread you will have a better idea of what this connection is about.

Cards 1, 2, 3, and 4 are dealing with the now, the and, the root, the last ten days. With the fifth card we see the possible consequence of an action not yet in full effect.

As we come to the sixth card the reader is now entering the next ten days. The information given on the sixth card commences within twenty-four hours. At the time of the reading I suggest that you take a close look at the fifth card to see if there might be any negative connotation or tendency to hold back as far as the querent is concerned.

7. THE APPREHENSION I FEEL

In the seventh position the energy shifts toward the querent. The focus is directed toward the response or lack of response of the querent toward the question given. Look at the correspondence or connection between the third and seventh cards to get a deeper insight as to "how and what" the querent is feeling.

The key to the seventh position is "the apprehension I feel." To help the querent understand his or her own hesitation regarding the issue, the reader can try to reinforce a positive outlook on any self-doubt or insecurity regarding the query.

8. THE FEELINGS OF OTHERS

This represents the input, the support, opinion, and point of view of those who may be involved, concerned, or interested in the querent's issue. The eighth card can give insight as to how others may be reacting to the querent's intentions or plans. As you look further into these areas of possibility you can then help to determine whether or not the querent is aware, or feels the support (or any obvious lack of support) in this situation.

9. THE POSITIVE ASPECT

The energy of the ninth card sheds light on the actual reason for the querent's question. The remaining and proceeding cards in the spread will clue you in to what is going on. For example, how the querent really feels and the measure of expectation by all concerned.

Consider the actual reason for the querent's question. As the spread begins to unfold you can then observe what and if there are any obstacles that could prevent the querent from achieving a satisfactory conclusion.

10. EXPECTED RESULTS WITHIN NEXT THIRTY DAYS

The tenth card gives an idea of what the querent can expect as a result of the question asked. All of the cards in the spread contribute to the tenth card.

The final conclusion has to be based on a combination of the nine preceding cards.

Consider the first nine cards as a base. From there you should be able to build upon and understand why the client asked the question and whether or not the reading presented a satisfactory conclusion.

DAILY RECORD BOOK

DATE: _____ TIME: _____

TYPE OF SPREAD: _____

QUESTION: _____

MAJOR/MINOR PACK: _____

List cards in order of spread.   SKETCH SPREAD OR NOTES:

_____

_____

_____

_____

_____

_____

_____

_____

_____

_____

INTERPRETATION OF SPREAD:

_____

_____

_____

_____

_____

_____

_____

_____

_____

DAILY RECORD BOOK

DATE: _____TIME: _____

TYPE OF SPREAD: _____

QUESTION: _____

MAJOR/MINOR PACK: _____

List cards in order of spread.   SKETCH SPREAD OR NOTES:

_____

_____

_____

_____

_____

_____

_____

_____

_____

_____

INTERPRETATION OF SPREAD:

_____

_____

_____

_____

_____

_____

_____

_____

_____

DAILY RECORD BOOK

DATE: _____TIME: _____

TYPE OF SPREAD: _____

QUESTION: _____

MAJOR/MINOR PACK: _____

List cards in order of spread.   SKETCH SPREAD OR NOTES:

_____

_____

_____

_____

_____

_____

_____

_____

_____

_____

INTERPRETATION OF SPREAD:

_____

_____

_____

_____

_____

_____

_____

_____

_____

_____

DAILY RECORD BOOK

DATE: _____TIME: _____

TYPE OF SPREAD: _____

QUESTION: _____

MAJOR/MINOR PACK: _____

List cards in order of spread.   SKETCH SPREAD OR NOTES:

_____

_____

_____

_____

_____

_____

_____

_____

_____

_____

INTERPRETATION OF SPREAD:

_____

_____

_____

_____

_____

_____

_____

_____

_____

DAILY RECORD BOOK

DATE: _____TIME: _____

TYPE OF SPREAD: _____

QUESTION: _____

MAJOR/MINOR PACK: _____

List cards in order of spread.   SKETCH SPREAD OR NOTES:

_____

_____

_____

_____

_____

_____

_____

_____

_____

_____

INTERPRETATION OF SPREAD:

_____

_____

_____

_____

_____

_____

_____

_____

_____

DAILY RECORD BOOK

DATE: _____TIME: _____

TYPE OF SPREAD: _____

QUESTION: _____

MAJOR/MINOR PACK: _____

List cards in order of spread.   SKETCH SPREAD OR NOTES:

_____

_____

_____

_____

_____

_____

_____

_____

_____

_____

INTERPRETATION OF SPREAD:

_____

_____

_____

_____

_____

_____

_____

_____

DAILY RECORD BOOK

DATE: _____TIME: _____

TYPE OF SPREAD: _____

QUESTION: _____

MAJOR/MINOR PACK: _____

List cards in order of spread.   SKETCH SPREAD OR NOTES:

_____

_____

_____

_____

_____

_____

_____

_____

_____

_____

INTERPRETATION OF SPREAD:

_____

_____

_____

_____

_____

_____

_____

_____

_____

DAILY RECORD BOOK

DATE: _____TIME: _____

TYPE OF SPREAD: _____

QUESTION: _____

MAJOR/MINOR PACK: _____

List cards in order of spread.   SKETCH SPREAD OR NOTES:

_____

_____

_____

_____

_____

_____

_____

_____

_____

_____

INTERPRETATION OF SPREAD:

_____

_____

_____

_____

_____

_____

_____

_____

_____

DAILY RECORD BOOK

DATE: _____ TIME: _____

TYPE OF SPREAD: _____

QUESTION: _____

MAJOR/MINOR PACK: _____

List cards in order of spread.   SKETCH SPREAD OR NOTES:

_____

_____

_____

_____

_____

_____

_____

_____

_____

_____

INTERPRETATION OF SPREAD:

_____

_____

_____

_____

_____

_____

_____

_____

_____

DAILY RECORD BOOK

DATE: _____TIME: _____

TYPE OF SPREAD: _____

QUESTION: _____

MAJOR/MINOR PACK: _____

List cards in order of spread.   SKETCH SPREAD OR NOTES:

_____

_____

_____

_____

_____

_____

_____

_____

_____

_____

INTERPRETATION OF SPREAD:

_____

_____

_____

_____

_____

_____

_____

_____

_____